Worlds of Care

Worlds of Care

THE EMOTIONAL LIVES OF FATHERS
CARING FOR CHILDREN WITH DISABILITIES

Aaron J. Jackson

UNIVERSITY OF CALIFORNIA PRESS

University of California Press
Oakland, California

© 2021 by Aaron J. Jackson

Library of Congress Cataloging-in-Publication Data

Names: Jackson, Aaron J., 1981– author.
Title: Worlds of care : the emotional lives of fathers caring for children
    with disabilities / Aaron J. Jackson.
Other titles: California series in public anthropology.
Identifiers: LCCN 2020037019 (print) | LCCN 2020037020 (ebook) | ISBN
    9780520379855 (cloth) | ISBN 9780520976955 (ebook)
Subjects: LCSH: Fathers of children with disabilities.
Classification: LCC HQ759.913 .J35 2021 (print) | LCC HQ759.913
    (ebook) | DDC 649/.151—dc23
LC record available at https://lccn.loc.gov/2020037019
LC ebook record available at https://lccn.loc.gov/2020037020

Manufactured in the United States of America

29 28 27 26 25 24 23 22 21 20
10 9 8 7 6 5 4 3 2 1

For Takoda

Contents

Acknowledgments

I owe much to the fathers and families who invited me into their lives and generously trusted me with their stories. I have been profoundly touched by their wisdom and generosity.

I want to thank Professor Tamara Kohn of Melbourne University's anthropology department, for going above and beyond the call of duty to support me through graduate school, for helping me strengthen my writing, and most importantly, for your friendship. I thank Professor Andrew Dawson, who inspired and encouraged me early on to keep writing. I want to thank the reviewers of this book for offering their suggestions and encouragement, including Professor Greg Downey of Macquarie University for his careful and detailed comments and Professor Maurice Hamington of Portland State University, whose enthusiasm with respect to the project touched me and whose work has immeasurably shaped my own.

I would also like to thank Professor Bob Simpson and Professor Tom Shakespeare for their helpful comments on an earlier iteration of this work.

A special thank you to Acquisitions Editor Kate Marshal and Enrique Ochoa-Kaup at the University of California Press for their early support and for shepherding my book through the approval and production process.

Love to Takoda's maternal grandparents, Nan and Poppy, for always cherishing his uniqueness.

I want to thank my mom for encouraging me to follow my own path.

Thanks to my younger sister for her openness, love, and humor.

There is no person in the world whom I owe more to than my partner, Kimberley Jamieson, whose care and labor have made this book possible. She was there for all the triumphs, pain, sorrow, and challenges that were part of this project from its inception until its final iteration as a book. I have no greater respect for any person on this earth. Her intellectual curiosity, fortitude, compassion, and care constantly remind me that we contain multitudes. Kimmy, I couldn't have done any of this as elegantly if you weren't by my side. I want to thank India and Winter, my daughters, for putting up with me during all the hours I have been caught up in my own world and showing me every day how easy it is to love. Finally, this book is for Takoda, my greatest teacher of all. You taught me to think and act differently. You taught me the meaning of care and how to live.

1 The Practice of Care

I was anxious meeting Pearl for the first time. I didn't want to say the wrong thing. Paul had already mentioned to me on a number of occasions that he finds it disconcerting when people ask Pearl questions she's not capable of answering. "What if she can understand the question," he said. "Don't you think it's cruel to ask her something when she has no way of communicating a response?" I had simply never thought about it before. For me, this style of communication is habit. Like Pearl, my son, Takoda, is nonverbal, and I suspect he has very limited receptive language—but there's no real way of telling. I often ask him questions as a matter of routine: "How was kindergarten, Takky? Did you have a good day?" My questioning is stitched into the rhythm of our interactions. I think my utterances, intonation, and pacing have meaning for him. But I absolutely understood Paul's point, which made me worry I was going to botch things up with Pearl. In the car on the way to his place I must have rehearsed in my mind at least a dozen times what I was going to say to her, making sure there were no questions.

With a polite smile I stepped into the cramped living room of their single-family home, where Pearl sat in her wheelchair. She was firmly striking the keys of a toy musical keyboard atop her wheelchair tray.

"Hi, Pearl. I'm Aaron," I said, and knelt down beside her. "I'm going to stay here with you and your dad for a bit while I do some research. He's told me so much about you."

With her head lowered and bent to one side, she glanced at me sideways with a smile that raised her cheeks, exposing big white teeth, which had the immediate effect of making me feel more relaxed. Foolishly, I thought I'd compose a short tune on her keyboard as a kind of bonding exercise. She shot me a sharply critical glance. So, with resigned humility, I settled for spectator status.

Lying awake in bed that night, I recognized my life in Pearl's fussing and yelling, which filled the house and filtered into my bedroom, breaking the dead silence, and in the sound of Paul's pacing footsteps outside my bedroom door as he opened and closed cupboards and rattled drawers. Anxiety around Takoda's disability cropped up in the furrows of my mind. I thought of how very little I had brought with me from my previous life to equip me for this one, as his caregiver. Although he was only four, sufficient uncertainty and distress had already been occasioned for me to know that I was living a life that felt deeply out of sync with the life I had lived and the lives of those around me. Pearl was twenty-two years old, eighteen years older than Takoda, and yet for Paul there seemed to be no end to the confusion, distress, and noise associated with his life as her caregiver. The truth is, I had been feeling badly about what I perceived to be my inadequacies as a father for some time. I was living with a gnawing uncertainty in what felt like a deeply ambiguous and ungrounded world. Finally, the house fell silent again.

Instead of going back to sleep, I sat in Paul's kitchen in the dark and gazed out the window at the dark foliage fringing the back of the house. Forlorn trees with heavy, somber branches swayed gracefully in the wind, ghostly figures in the light of the half-moon. Disability has become a fact of life and routine for Paul. But far from being something he takes for granted, the everyday seems like something of an achievement, unfolding against a background of uncertainty and in relation to demands that clash with the imperatives of control and autonomy. Sitting there in the pre-dawn silence, I recalled a story he told me, not too long ago. It was about his visit with the school district superintendent right after the discovery that Pearl had been sexually assaulted. That had been six years ago. Paul had found evidence clearly suggesting she'd been sexually abused some-time during school hours. A criminal investigation was launched, but it failed to find the person responsible. The incident powered a profound despair that still gripped him and posed a direct threat to his trust in oth-ers. In trying to win the sympathy of those in attendance at the school meeting to discuss the incident and evoke thoughtful consideration of his situation with Pearl, I believe Paul was trying to convey something about the uncertainties of their everyday life together and its precarious achievement. That is to say, while their life is beset by health crises and frightening seizures, they find some measure of control and security over the impersonal forces that lie beyond us through successful interactions of trust with others, an ongoing achievement that violence and prejudice can destroy at any moment.

He was sitting in the school district superintendent's office, along with the assistant superintendent for student services, the director of special education, and Pearl's mother. Despite the magnitude of the situation, there was a calm dignity softening the edges of his anger and despair.

He looked the superintendent straight in the eye and said, "Listen, I bet you and I start every day the same. Every morning I wake up, wiggle my toes, stretch, and get out of bed. Okay?"

The superintendent nodded in agreement.

"Then I put on a robe and slippers," Paul said.

More nodding.

"Every morning, for twenty years, I walk down the hall and into my daughter's room to check that she's still alive and hasn't died in the middle of the night."

Silence.

THE VERTIGO OF EXISTENTIAL DISRUPTION

Existential disruption refers to an experience of profound disorientation that can make it hard to know how to go on or make sense of one's life. "To become disoriented," as the philosopher Ami Harbin writes, "is, roughly, to lose one's bearings in relation to others, environments, and life projects."[1] The site of disruption is one's world. Specifically, disruption is experienced through profound disturbances to self- experience and understanding, lived time, and relatedness to others.[2] Upon entering their worlds of disability, many parents have no understanding of their new situations as caregivers. They are often at a loss, not knowing what to make of and with the world of which they are suddenly part. One father I met described his arrival moment as a "monumental life-changing situation that parents come to with no basis of reality." Another said, "It is so overwhelming. Your life is completely turned upside down and absolutely readjusted in a way that affects everything you do, all your ambitions."

Disruption tears people from their absorption in a familiar world and incites a confrontation with the unfamiliar. It is a mode of existence connected to the subjective experience of self-continuity across time. As psychiatrist and philosopher Thomas Fuchs tells us, because it is habitual, "the lived body exhibits a specific form of memory that results from the continual embodiment of existence."[3] Every new experience rests upon a background of affinities, expectations, attitudes, experiences, and capacities acquired in the course of a life.[4] These aspects form a horizon that prefigures our current understanding and contextualizes experience, motivating the articulation of particular significances and concerns. Thus, the lived body conveys a "feeling of sameness," as Fuchs puts it, or a "felt constancy of subjectivity," by integrating the past in one's present being and potentiality.[5] Self-familiarity, then, gives us a view of the future. Or, as phenomenologist Maurice Merleau-Ponty expresses it, "My world is carried forward by lines of intentionality which trace out in advance at least the style of what is to come."[6] Disruption is an expression of a temporal disjunction between past (and its future) and present; a disjunction in the order of time. It gives rise to a feeling of disequilibrium, wherein the past with all the future anticipations it carries continues to bleed into the present unabated, often leading people to ask, "What shall I do now?" Regaining a sense of equilibrium, then, rests on the continual project of knitting the past and future together.

Disruption also takes cultural and structural root as it is shaped by age-related behavioral norms and shared social practices, as well as by societal values and behaviors that reflect and shape expressions of social prejudice against people with disabilities. Western culture tends to emphasize independence and autonomy as values, which then permeate our conceptions of the good life and affect deeply how parents experience and respond to having a child who may require a high level of care for the rest of their lives. Furthermore, Western cultural ideas about biography, choice, progress, order, linearity, and temporal coherence reflect people's changing concerns, expectations, self-understanding, and priorities. Our grasp of the normative life course is shaped by these ideas and gives a powerful ordering to life so that disorienting events can prompt profoundly disruptive effects.

By deviating from the normative course of life, parents caring for children with severe disabilities find themselves out of step with the norms and practices of others in the community. This can lead to their feeling excluded from cultural lifecycle events, as well as to having fewer people to share their experiences with from social life more broadly. Indeed, for many such parents, unexpected hospital stays, watching their children fail to meet typical developmental and social milestones, fighting for services and for their child's rights, repeated surgeries, and participating in early intervention services can involve an ongoing conversation with an embittered form of social alienation. Creating a meaningful life thus involves reckoning with an experience of dwelling in incommensurate worlds.

Parents arrive to their worlds of disability by different routes, but invariably the taken-for-granted rhythm of life is broken. For philosopher Alfred Schutz and sociologist Thomas Luckman, the experience of a breakdown of the routines of daily life prompts a change of attitude toward reality, a break with one's familiar acceptance of the world. "Familiar," they write, "is usually graspable only in the negative, through 'effects of alienation,' which occur when something hitherto familiar suddenly 'explodes.'"[7] What problems and potentials arise from this confrontation with the unfamiliar? For parents, moving from a sense of unfamiliar to the familiar requires careful cultivation.

In this book, I am especially interested in the experiences of men caring for children with major cognitive and physical disabilities, for both the literature on caregiving and cultural texts about disruption often elide these experiences. Fatherhood is often taken as simply a patriarchal backdrop against which other accounts of gender, kinship, and care are played out. Studies that explore fatherhood in its own right are still relatively uncommon; ones that deal with fathers as caregivers even less so. How do they find some kind of normal with their children when the wider settings in which they exist render them as anything but? What possibilities, if any, does the moral experience of caregiving offer for one's life and ethical cultivation?

LIVING WITH DISRUPTION

When it comes to disability and serious illness, disruption is a familiar theme. Many anthropological and sociological studies have examined the cultural shape of disruption and emphasized people's attempts at finding meaning in the aftermath of change. In this book I examine worlds of care among fathers of children with major cognitive and developmental disabilities. I bring into focus the profound disjunction experienced by fathers upon the arrival of such a child and the ongoing impacts and adjustments that must be made or resisted as the child grows up. The demands both of caregiving and of achieving the level of responsivity that is needed in the non-self-interested labor that characterizes it can place tremendous burdens on caregivers. Many of the men in this book will never hear the words "thank you" or "I love you, dad." Caring for a child that is not capable of normative reciprocity, often expressed in language or reciprocal eye contact, and that will never achieve and experience the developmental and social milestones that parents typically anticipate, can amplify anguish and disorientation. Parents are left to contend, simply, with what is. It is the sheer level of complexity and responsibility at the heart of caregiving that makes it stand out in such a marked way.

My interest in addressing how caring for children with disabilities impacts families and individuals is grounded in my life as a caregiver for my son. My new life of practice as his caregiver started in the summer of 2011 when he began having frightening tonic-clonic (grand mal) seizures. He was only a baby then, four months old, in fact. At first, he was diagnosed with global developmental delay; sometime later, he was declared severely intellectually disabled. Flummoxed and disoriented, I found myself adrift in seas of strangeness. I no longer felt that I clearly understood my life. Whatever privilege my shell of comfort as a white able-bodied male afforded me moving within and between people and settings without fear of exclusion or discrimination was violently cracked open. My son's body became a curious public spectacle in even the most prosaic spaces of daily life, and I felt this as palpably as though it were my own. Hearing the word "retard" muttered by a stranger made my bones quake with a feeling I had never experienced before. The truth is, my son's disabilities revealed a world that had been secretly nestled inside the one I had so blithely inhabited. I wondered how many of these realities are nestled inside one another, like nesting dolls, revealed or obscured in accordance with how we exist in the world. I wanted to know how I was supposed to reconcile my life with this new one and the precarious and restricted future it hinted at.

Within a few months of reading other accounts by parents, I came to realize that my experience of unexpected disruption reflected a common theme in the lives of caregivers. This became the springboard for my study and compelled me to carry out research into the embodied experiences of men—fathers like me—caring for children with major physical and intellectual disabilities. I desperately needed to know how they come to understand these unexpected changes to their lives and strive to make livable worlds with their children.

This book is a meditation on fathers' everyday lived experiences surrounding care and the moral personhood of their severely disabled children. Grounded in both my personal experience as a caregiver and ethnographic fieldwork carried out in the United Sates in 2015, this book is concerned with how fathers go about creating what I call "habitable worlds" after the existential disruption spurred by the major life shift of having a child that falls outside of what is considered species typical. I explore the concrete lives of men fathering disabled children, connecting the cultural experience of caregiving to the changing mediums of experience and existential conditions it is rooted in. In effect, I have written a book I wish I had been able to read back when Takoda was a baby.

What is perhaps new in my approach and thinking about care is my turn toward embodiment and personal experience.[8] From the inception of my research, my presence pervades the details of this book. My familiarity with the lived world of caregiving gives me direct insight not only into the mundane activities that comprise giving care but also into the conflict, uncertainty, quandaries, and intimacy it brings into play. Through caring for my son I am aware of the way the experience and practice of caregiving can call caregivers to be present in new ways and enhance life's meaning, while at the same time exposing "troubling truths about what it means to be human."[9] Like others in this book, my story is one of embodied disruption. Thus, the inclusion of myself is another way that embodied experience makes an impact in this book. The ongoing discoveries and disclosures that lie at the heart of my experiences caring for Takoda provided important insights that have guided my observations, interpretations, and interactions with fathers, for example, my focus on how they gain certain kinds of access to the inner lives of their children or discover complementary ways of acting. My story is therefore inseparable from the picture that emerges in this book of how fathers create their worlds of care. By focusing on how fathers reorient their lives and find new meanings through different registers of experience and mediums of engagement with their children, my approach offers a bracing realism that qualifies heavily how we think of personhood, disability, and moral agency.

CAREGIVING, FATHERING, AND MASCULINITY

This is a book about men and caregiving—specifically the work of fathers caring for children with major physical and cognitive disabilities in America. Several aspects make this form of caregiving distinctive: the complexity, protracted and morally demanding nature, and intimacy of care provided. As sociologist Gillian Ranson notes in relation to caregiving more generally, it is usually mothers, not fathers, who are recognized as doing most of this informal labor.[10] The reasons for this are embedded in societal and cultural understandings about how men and women, as fathers and mothers, should think and behave. Therefore, the link between masculinities and caring is an important one. Given that most prevailing dominant cultural forms of masculinity are "largely associated with a devaluation of the feminine while caring is often equated with feminine practice,"[11] men's caregiving experiences need to be partially contextualized by a consideration of how they think and feel about themselves as fathers in relation to dominant conceptions of masculinity, or what gender theorist R. W. Connell describes as the most celebrated or "honoured way of being a man" in a particular social setting.[12] Dominant masculine ideals provide cultural reference points for the ways men ought to relate to themselves and think and behave toward others.

A focus on fathers' embodied experiences of caregiving requires an exploration of how their experiences are mediated by their already existing relation to the world and ongoing embodied interactions with others. In a nutshell, this exploration involves what it is that fathers are actually doing in the care of their children and a focus on the inner resonance of particular moments and events, which can serve as a window into their deepest feelings. A focus of this kind necessarily throws into relief moments of being that expose norms of gendered embodiment, their practice, and implications.

This book extends the boundaries of care to make visible the embodied experiences of men involved in what is sometimes referred to as "extreme caregiving"[13] and explores how their histories of gendered embodiment bear on their experiences of caregiving. Rather than reducing men to exemplars of different types of masculinities, I am interested in the relationship between their sexed and gendered bodies and embodied emotional histories. I describe everyday experiences in order to reveal some of the unquestioned presuppositions and values about everyday life that mediate fathers' expectations and understandings about particular events and situations, which help constitute a context that articulates the significance of an event or situation.

My starting point for a consideration of the link between the embodied character of fathers' caregiving experiences and dominant gender norms is grounded in my own life and the ways my childhood and relationships prepared or failed to prepare me for the eventualities I go on to describe. The experience of caregiving and fathering cannot be disaggregated from the changing personal and emotional worlds that provide the grounds for a powerful sense of who we are and what we should be doing and that guide the ways parents find themselves morally oriented in the world as caregivers. We "grow into a customary interpretation of ourselves and grow up on that interpretation," to invoke existential philosopher Martin Heidegger's famous dictum.[14] Instead of continuing to focus on the structural conditions that support and nurture greater fatherhood involvement as so much of the literature on fatherhood has done, I emphasize the way everyday feelings, actions, and words embody an interpretation of who we are, albeit one that is often covered up by its habitual character, and how this opens certain possibilities for fathering projected in the ways men understand their lives. In this regard, I see dominant and persisting gender norms and ideologies as part of the factual conditions of ethical life. "There is not a part of its warp and woof into which they have not entered," to borrow philosopher William Barret's words.[15] So while it is arguable that fatherhood and manhood are separate constructs, at the level of lived experience I find they are not so easily teased apart.

MAKING CONTACT WITH THE PEOPLE IN THE STUDY

My wife, Kim, Takoda, and our daughter India joined me on the fieldwork I undertook for this book. I began the research in Phoenix, Arizona, after contacting Earl, the founder of a support group for men caring for disabled children, and who ran monthly meetings across metropolitan Phoenix (locally referred to as the Valley). At the time, Earl was on the cusp of retirement—a married white male in his late fifties who worked as an engineer/paramedic with the fire department. Earl established the support group some fourteen years earlier, when his disabled son, Zachary, was fourteen. My family and I arrived and settled in Scottsdale, an affluent suburb northeast of downtown Phoenix, at the beginning of a record-setting heatwave that lingered over the sprawling desert metropolis for three weeks. During those first weeks, I recruited several men from Earl's support meetings into the study.

Early on, support meetings seemed like a sensible way to access fathers. From the preliminary research I had conducted back home in Australia, support groups for men caring for children with severe developmental disabilities were scarce to nonexistent in that country. But my early impression of his thriving support group proved erroneous, as Earl's meetings also suffered severely from a lack of attendance. During my first meeting, for example, only one other person attended. During the second, at a different location, there were four of us: me, Earl, and two other guys he has known for over a decade. There was no set agenda. We sat around a long table on the outdoor patio of an IHOP restaurant conversing on a range of subjects, but no one talked about their children or home life.

At first, I attributed their reticence to my presence as a stranger. After a while it dawned on me that the group mostly comprised men who had friendships dating back many years. It seemed they had created a space of acceptance and comfort around their similar identities as caregivers and commonalities of experience. But these things were rarely, if ever, thematized in discussion. Instead, the connection between them was present in moments of laughter and palpable in the knowing silences they shared. They didn't come to meetings to share advocacy tips and care strategies, or to ask for and give help and advice to one another. It was this sense of sharedness that brought them together. As one father later remarked, "It's a good feeling to be around people you've known for a while and that you don't have to explain everything to." Most of them had children who were grown or well into their teenage years. If they had ever needed to openly communicate their experiences and share tips, that time had passed.

In the beginning recruitment to my study depended on the people Earl put me in contact with. Over time, however, it became clear that his potential to connect me with others had been stretched to its limits, so I met fathers in other ways. For example, an organization in southern Arizona that provides training programs for parents of children with disabilities sent out an announcement about my research to those on their electronic mailing list. I also spent time with fathers I had come to know about through their online blogs or published essays.[16] I also spoke with partners, wives, siblings, friends, teachers, home health aides, and therapists that fathers introduced me to.

My inclusion criteria were broad. The men in this book care for children who range in age from four to twenty-six years. Their diagnoses vary—sensory, intellectual, physical—as do their needs. Despite the variation in differences, however, they all require a high level of hands-on care and are considered by their respective caregivers as severely or profoundly disabled. In the end, eight men participated in my study. Most of them live in Maricopa County in Arizona. One father resides in Ohio, while another lives in Massachusetts. Thus, this is an individual-centered and multi-sited study.

My field of study slowly emerged through time around the individuals who invited me into their lives. It comprises individuals who share a common history in relation to their children, a history that speaks to the negative cultural value ascribed to their children's embodied differences and their separation from able-bodied culture. Participants were born in the United States and are predominately Anglo-American, though there is some diversity, as one participant is Jewish and another is Latino. All of them come from working-class or middle-class backgrounds. Some have undergraduate or graduate degrees, while others served in the military or pursued trade school. These fathers share identities as caregivers, identities that generate the kinds of motivations and loyalties that constitute communities, whether they are interacting with each another or not.

Interestingly, it is not uncommon to hear people ask about men who cannot cope with the demands of caregiving and abandon their families. That so many are curious about this phenomenon is interesting in itself. My book, however, tightly focuses on the much less explored topic of how fathers render their worlds habitable after disruption.

AN EXPERIENTIAL PERSON-CENTERED APPROACH TO CAREGIVING

It is in the moral practice of giving care, in the doing, thinking, and feeling, that fathers come to understand their lives and those around them. It is in the practical, mundane activities of daily living that caregivers negotiate their constantly changing, diverse worlds of disability as embodied subjects in time and space with others. This book considers the most significant aspects of caregivers' worlds as experienced by them. My focus on care, embodiment, and the existential grounds that constitute fathers' possibilities for giving care offers a corrective to anthropological approaches that elevate the conceptual and linguistic dimensions of human existence. With respect to the children represented in this book, these approaches are inadequate and create considerable problems, because they overlook how children with severe disabilities actively inhabit their worlds and affect those around them.

I share existential anthropology's commitment to exploring the empirical lives of "actual people in everyday situations."[17] My research exhibits a strong focus on singular individuals with a view to compare beings in the process of existing across time and reorienting their lives as caregivers. This focus involves a "shift away from socio-perspectivism," to borrow existential anthropologist Albert Piette's words, toward "an anthroperspectivism that seeks to describe human existence, its continuity in time."[18]

My study has as one of its precedents an interest within anthropology in how individuals experience their worlds after some kind of disruption and how the forces of language, history, and upbringing are given meaning and find expression as individuals strive to regain a sense of equilibrium.[19] For anthropologist Michael Jackson, disruption "lays people open to possibilities of behavior that they embody as potentialities but ordinarily are not inclined to express."[20] The past three decades have given rise to fruitful studies that examine issues of politics and power in the realms of medicine, technology, gender, and the body. What seems lacking in the literature on caregiving in the context of disability is some explicit consideration of the mediums of experience and modes of meaningful engagement and relationality involved in the ways people come to know themselves and shape the worlds into which they are thrown.

Maurice Merleau-Ponty's work has greatly influenced my thinking on relationality, especially the idea that relation characterizes our life from its very start. This is now evinced by studies on infant imitation, whereby newborns are shown to be in possession of a rudimentary ability to monitor their own gestures and recognize and imitate the gestures and expressions of others.[21] Studies like these revise and refine Merleau-Ponty's earlier theorizing about the dialogic structure of subjectivity by providing empirical support for the theory of an innate body schema that accounts for the possibility of a self in relation to others.[22] Therefore, a significant part of this book focuses on the variety of ways experience is made accessible and mediated through interpersonal and intersubjective encounters. As you will see, this book approaches culture and parents' experiences of caring from a relational perspective, that is to say, from the perspective that we always understand ourselves in relation to others and shared practices. Being-in-the-world-with others, as Heidegger puts it, is a necessary condition for our coming into consciousness as subjects.[23] Simply put, there is an "intersubjective significance" to our perceptions.[24]

My approach emphasizes that the experience of being embodied is mediated by our interactions with others.[25] "Even in our most individual and private consciousness," philosopher Jean Wahl writes, "we are not separated from others."[26] For example, this can be glimpsed in the way disruption is experienced by parents as a changed lived relation to themselves and the world. Parents reflexively negotiate their identities as caregivers alongside other multi-perspectival views, both in relation to their ever-changing memories of other people and the information reflected back to them as caregivers in interaction.

I lean on Merleau-Ponty's embodiment theory to understand the way fathers as bodily subjects forge and develop a sense of themselves across time and in relation to others. His expansion of the body schema is a key concept with which to consider the body's potential for learning and exercising care and how caring knowledge and habits can reconfigure the boundary conditions of perception and action. I also cite Maurice Hamington's theory on embodied care throughout the text, which provides a rich resource for thinking about how care is facilitated by the human body and the affective, embodied, and intercorporeal grounds upon which we exercise our imaginative abilities to empathize with others, especially those outside our own sphere of experience.[27]

In my approach, I have sought to capture the seemingly prosaic details of daily life and small gestures that hint at personal histories of bodily practice and interaction of fathers in the process of living with their children. I became interested in the kind of automaticity related to habits and practices that speak to the experiences and capacities a person has acquired throughout their life, like the time I watched a father intensely arguing with someone all the while feeding his adult son a plate of pancakes, being attentive to him through minor gestures of care. These habits of attention and responsive actions provide glimpses into fathers' histories of embodied experience, sedimented in specific skills and operative at any given moment.

There were other details I focused on too: awkward or eloquent silences, heavy pauses, laughter, and affective dispositions. These details are inextricably tied to people's states of mind, desires, underlying moods and feelings, and other aspects of consciousness, including self-experience and memory. Paying attention to these sorts of details can provide glimpses into how the present experience resonates within the longer-term framework of a person's life.[28] I frequently brought these observed details into conversation with my participants, and by getting an individual's own detailed description or explanation of certain actions and gestures, I was able to supplement and deepen my observations. These unconventional features of my research design turned out to be instrumental in identifying what matters most to fathers in the course of their lives.

In this book, caregiving emerges as an experience profoundly connected to the existential possibilities that, to borrow from Heidegger, we choose, grow up in, stumble into, or develop over time.[29] These possibilities are grounded in the changing ways caregivers understand themselves across time, their affective and emotional ties to their children, and the full range of meanings, memories, perceptions, feelings, thoughts, and actions available to them. My attempt to illuminate the ways men make what they can of themselves and their worlds, within limits, draws inspiration from Heidegger's concept of the human being as a self-interpreter. In simple and less abstract terms, we are always pressing ahead into the future in relation to a particular understanding of ourselves that is embedded in conditions not of our choosing, for example, place and time, and my body and past. In other words, we find ourselves disclosed in a historical and cultural way, situated by ethnicity, religion, place of birth, and gender, with a particular past and body, caught up in everyday life and tuned in to situations. Therefore, we act and exist in accordance with the ways the world is made meaningful to us in our attunement.[30] We are "attuned," as philosopher William Blattner puts it, "to what makes certain ways of being worthwhile, fun, desirable, scary, noble, exhilarating, and so on."[31] Our ability to be, therefore, is governed by what it's like for something to be the way it is.

In the case of parents, disruption arises from a struggle to unify past, present, and future. That is to say, the experience of disruption directly implicates the past and future as well as the present, throwing into relief the temporal dimensions of caregiving. By focusing on how the normal and habitual is disrupted and experienced by fathers after having a disabled child, and the links of disruption to complex processes of selfhood and identification, my research revealed that fathers' possibilities for remaking their lives are bound up in particular biographical significances.

Caregivers' experiences, then, are impossible to speak about without invoking a sense of their lived personal histories. These existential possibilities go a long way in explaining how responses to caregiving differ so much across individuals.

For example, while my role as a young father fostered the kind of intimacy that gave me access to participants' private lives and lent itself to the emotional disclosures I was interested in, my shifts in identity from father to researcher sometimes jarred with their expectations, which at times had a cooling effect on relationships. For example, Earl, who was crucial in facilitating my introductions to other men early on, aligned his passion project of recording fathers' testimonies about the power of positive fathering with my research. He asked me to record my conversations with fathers so that he could upload them to his website as a resource to help others. I told him that his agenda was different from my own. I explained my concerns about how a cameraman would impinge upon the privacy and conduct of those I was spending time with. Apparently offended, he withdrew from contact with me.

It was during this time that I decided to reach out to fathers from outside the support group. The situation provoked anxiety within me and I found myself reacting strongly. I was reeling with ambivalence—the anthropologist part of me wanted to reach out and reconcile things by offering to conduct interviews for Earl's website (as a side project to my own), but another part of me felt wronged and mindful of the paternalism at play. This event was cause for further emotional introspection. It made me realize that my feelings were tied to my past, to growing up under my father's paternalism and abuse. Thereafter, emotions became integral to my research for their epistemic value. As I cast an analytical eye on personal habits and assumptions, repressed feelings and motives sometimes erupted to the surface, alongside other uncomfortable dualities. I began journaling my feelings and discussing them with Kim, which helped deepen my interpretations of what was going on and separate my own experience and concerns from those of my participants. Contemplating these emotions during fieldwork gave birth to new lines of thought and inquiry. For instance, this episode with Earl drew my attention to gender-based styles of communicating and relating to others.

A PUBLIC FORM OF PERSONAL CARING

"Don't we need a benchmark to measure what we are?" a well-known scholar once asked me. I had just delivered a paper on disability and caregiving at an annual academic conference. The paper was based on a recognition of the wide spectrum of human variation and put forth an expansive notion of community and citizenship. It was largely inspired by my life caring for Takoda and informed by what I have come to know of his sensorial experiences and how they shape his being-in-the-world. I was engaged in what can be thought of as a cosmopolitan form of activism, arguing that the just treatment of those with severe intellectual and physical disabilities should be based on a recognition of our interdependence as human beings. I wanted to shine a light on the othering practices that foreclose our capacity to connect with and understand others.[32] When it came time to the Q&A afterward, however, my ability to think and all of the linguistic powers I had been honing since childhood collapsed into a heap of visceral rumblings, and so it was with this scholar's follow-up question: "Why should we do this moral work [valuing Takoda and those like him as equal moral beings]?"

This line of questioning throws into relief a distinct tension between my dual role as an anthropologist and stakeholder in these wider debates around the moral personhood of those with severe developmental disabilities, namely, as a caregiver. It's not always easy to discuss Takoda's moral personhood in such detached and theoretical ways—after all, he is my son. Yet, this is my chosen area of expertise and so I must expect these critical rituals of argument and questioning because I am institutionally expected to indulge both reasonable and prolix questioning. But it is also more than this. It is what philosopher Eva Kittay calls a "public form of personal caring"; a part of the invisible labor that family members of disabled people sometimes engage in to socialize the world to meet their child.[33]

As a philosopher and mother of a severely intellectually disabled daughter, Kittay writes about an experience similar to mine at a bioethics conference, describing the profound emotional challenges she experiences when she is forced to respond to moral claims about the nonperson status of her daughter and those with cognitive disabilities like her. She writes, "How can I begin to tell you what it feels like to read texts in which one's child is compared, in all seriousness and with philosophical authority, to a dog, pig, rat, and most flattering a chimp; how corrosive these comparisons are, how they mock those relationships that affirm who we are and why we care?"[34]

Here, Kittay is specifically referring to the views of philosophers Peter Singer and Jeff McMahan, who hold an instrumental view of human life and contentiously demote the moral status of those with cognitive disabilities because of their perceived lack of certain psychological and/or moral capacities. As Kittay acknowledges, while for theorists the wedge may be mere abstraction, such disendowments have historically permitted the abuse and neglect of those with cognitive disabilities—which continues unabated in certain regions of the world today—and have the potential to translate into horrific consequences on a practical level via bioethics into healthcare and policy decisions.[35]

Kittay's perspective on care is based on a relational approach to personhood that defines our humanness in accordance with our connections and intrinsic interdependence; a view that directs our attention to the claim that relationships are constitutive of who we are. In her seminal work, *Love's Labor*, she offers one of the most cogent arguments for the social inclusion and moral treatment of those with profound cognitive disabilities within the realm of distributive justice. She amends John Rawls's theory of distributive justice to include care as a primary good by revisioning caregiving as a public good that promotes human flourishing. She argues that dependency is an inescapable dimension of human existence, attested to by infancy, childhood, illness, advanced age, and disability.[36] The networks of giving and receiving, or our "nested dependencies" as she phrases it, make us all worthy recipients of care.[37]

Kittay's argument calls us to recognize what should be a shared commitment to care for each other and society's obligation toward providing adequate provisions to support dependency relations. While I share with Kittay a concern for relations of care, I push the analysis in a different direction to illustrate an intensely mutual interdependence and interaffectivity by throwing light on the particular ways children with disabilities act upon their parents in ethically significant ways, beyond our dominant understandings of personhood and sociality. In doing so, this book describes the alternate ways those with severe intellectual disabilities affect and move those around them through emotional and bodily modes of agency.

This book resides somewhere between research and literature. It resonates with what anthropologist Clifford Geertz referred to as "faction": "imaginative writing about real people in real places at real times."[38] I employ creative nonfiction in different ways and for different reasons throughout this book, sometimes to condense large swathes of information and action into a digestible portrait, sometimes for the interpretive openness they allow. That is to say, rather than pinning down moments by imposing a particular reading on them, I invite the reader to vicariously inhabit the world of another. In these instances, I focus on emotions, atmospheres, and states of mind to capture how particular moments appear to and resonate with the people concerned. With regard to the children in this study, I hope these literary devices do service to their lives and the dignity of living without language and other cognitive capacities often taken to be the hallmarks of humanhood.

Each chapter poses a particular set of questions that, taken together, indicate a spectrum of issues faced by fathers and give insight into a socially and morally complex set of human interdependencies. Let me begin by laying out three claims, which can serve as signposts for what follows.

My argument begins with the claim that the demands of caregiving shake parents from their familiar worlds and launch them upon a new subjective trajectory, whereupon they struggle to remake a biographically coherent self in the context of care and disability. Their attempts to reorient their lives, therefore, are coextensive with the lives they have lived and the biographical significances they bring to bear in creating meaning and coping with their new situations as caregivers.

My second claim is that the body plays a fundamental role in facilitating what parents know about care and how they come to know it.

Third, caregiving experiences permeate fathers' self-understanding and life projects. Experiences of disorientation and the practice of care have the potential to contribute to their moral agency through the head-on exposure of normative social and cultural patterns that eschew caring, not only tearing the veil off unquestioned presuppositions about everyday life but refiguring the ways they perceive, interpret, and interact with the world and those around them in accordance with the ethical demands of caregiving. Thus, giving care can foster ethical cultivation and holds the promise of achieving moral change.

If we look at caregiving descriptively, then—that is, ethnographically in terms of what concrete caregiving entails and how it is experienced by fathers providing care—the embodied, situated, and emergent features of relational selfhood become central to understanding the significance of care and its articulation in moral life.

Finally, as a form of public personal caring, I hope this book contributes to the broader project of making more individuals aware of the diverse ways people inhabit the world and our capacity for care which exists in potential. In the end, I hope the various stories I seek to represent play the role of a welcome mat, inviting readers to openly encounter and identify with the lives of the people in this book across, and in spite of, difference. Through a deepened resonance with unfamiliar others we can begin creating more imaginative and relationally attuned living spaces. In their book, *Care Ethics and Poetry*, Hamington and Rosenow draw attention to the crucial role imagination and knowledge play in caring for others: it takes imagination to understand different social experiences and speculate about how our actions might impact others, and the more we know about others the greater our potential for empathy and compassion.[39] Perhaps this book can be a conduit for acquiring the kind of knowledge that can lead to more social and personal caring habits and responsive caring actions. It is my hope that the unfamiliar speaks in an intimate way, regardless of the reader's experience with disability and care of loved ones, providing a sense of how we cultivate our worlds and the complex habits of caring that nurture them and bring them out at their best.

A WORD ON DEFINITIONS

There is a lot of variation in the way disability is defined and approached. In this book, I approach disability from a phenomenological perspective that considers the body-in-the-world. The parents in this study are caring for children whose bodies and minds depart, quite radically, from what is considered socially and culturally normative. I approach disability as an intrinsic condition of human existence that is irreducibly connected to the way the world is disclosed through embodied existence while at the same time being conditioned by the world we are in (historical and social context, environment, relations of power, disabling barriers, and cultural values). There is resonance here with what disability studies scholar Tom Shakespeare has called a "relational approach" to understanding disability: the interrelatedness of both intrinsic and extrinsic factors that constitute disability.[40]

My approach to disability also informs the way I use the terms "fathers," "parents," and "caregivers" throughout this book. A research focus on bodiliness throws light on fathers' experiences of male embodiment. From an existential phenomenological perspective, I consider gender norms and practices as elements of culture and, therefore, factual conditions of existence. In this respect, I try to be sensitive to the ways I use these terms. For example, when I consider phenomena where gender differences seem inconsequential, I try to refer to the experiences of "parents" and "caregivers" to avoid the gender connotations associated with fatherhood—for example, the workings of memory, sympathetic perception, and affect are hardly the exclusive province of men. I use the term "fathers" when considering the gendered dimensions of existence or else when referring to the concrete realities of the men who are the subjects of this book.

OUTLINE OF THE BOOK

Worlds of Care has seven chapters. This introductory first chapter has sketched out the premise of the book and its distinctive focus on fathering, setting the stage upon which to explore how fathers create habitable worlds. I have also offered some background about my own story caring for a severely disabled child and described my research approach to investigating the role of identity formation and disruption in the context of caregiving.

The second chapter presents a series of what I call arrival stories, depicting how some of the men in this book arrived into their worlds of disability. The rest of the chapter explores the underexamined relevance of memories in understanding the experiential character of disruption and argues that by drawing on the depths and potentiality of the past the fathers in this book create new forms of self-understanding in the context of their lives as caregivers.

I then offer a brief interlude that introduces a new participant and offers another example of the ways parents in various contexts arrive to their worlds of disability.

The third chapter addresses the interbodily dimensions of caregiving and how fathers gain access to the inner lives of their children in the absence of normative reciprocity and communication. I explore the body's role in delivering care and how the acquisition of caring habits can enhance our connection to others, alter habits of consciousness, and refigure fathers' moral identities as caregivers.

The fourth chapter considers how men are morally oriented as fathers in relation to their histories of gendered experience and norms of masculinity. By zigzagging through several narratives, including an account of my own childhood and relationships, I show how these personal histories attune fathers to what morally matters in their experiences of caring for their children. These narrative recollections give important insights into fathers' later emotional responses and the personal and politicized steps some take toward creating more equitable relations with others in the service of creating inclusive realities for their children. It also brings in the idea of intersubjective breakdown as an experience that is particularly helpful in unveiling self-assumptions and interpretations embodied in our ways of behaving toward others, potentially shifting the ways men relate to notions of manhood, fatherhood, and care, humbly provoking moral change.

At the end of chapter 4 I offer an interlude: a brief story that moves the abstract idea of being-for-others (the theme in the following chapter) to concrete reality. Rather than offering a formalized explanation I prefer to articulate the emotional knowledge through the form of a story.

Chapter 5 considers experiences of embodied shame in everyday affective and social spaces where cultural meanings surrounding life and the body are negotiated and contested. I examine how our sense of relation to the world is impregnated by others and how moments of objectification threaten to collapse the interpersonal bridge between self and other. Experiences of shame offer insights into the springs and motives that propel fathers in their personal and collective attempts to refigure spaces of social activity and belonging.

In chapter 6 I focus on the moral personhood of disabled children and modes of agency overlooked in ascriptions of personhood dependent on language, reason, and self-consciousness. This necessarily involves a focus on embodied interaction and the social and emotional dimensions of their lives. I also investigate the situated demands of caregiving and the role moral intuitions play in defining individuals' and communities' ethical worlds, throwing into relief the differences, commonalities, and conflicts that arise between individuals and groups who hold diverging moral views. I conclude the chapter by introducing the notion of "moral cosmopolitanism," exploring the collaborative efforts parents engage in to expand the public's empathetic understanding and imaginative capacity for caring about those beyond their sphere of experience.

I conclude with an epilogue to offer some final thoughts.

2 The Depths of Time

PAST BECOMINGS AND HABITABLE WORLDS

Memory is the seamstress, and a capricious one at that.
Memory runs her needle in and out, up and down, hither
and thither. We know not what comes next, or what follows
after.

Virginia Woolf, *Orlando*

I was no more than six years old when my cousin Benji hurled Ossie out
the second-floor window of his house. Ossie lost both his eyes during the
fall. Afterward, someone filled them in with a black permanent marker.
I was upset because Ossie was special to me. Sometime before my third
birthday my parents had my "wandering eye" surgically corrected and he'd
been a great comfort before and after the procedure. Mom tells me my
memory is mistaken, and that Ossie was a reward for having the surgery.
I still have him, but now he's a bedraggled-looking bird who spends his
days in my daughter's toy chest. To this day, he reminds me of the lonely
hospital room, the boy who cried in the bed next to me—whose face has
been erased by time—and the nurse who comforted me on her lap. I can
only remember her white shoes, which I'm told I threw up on, and how
warm and safe I felt in her arms.

Benji was six years older than me at the time of Ossie's accident.
I couldn't fathom what I had done to provoke his actions. He was the
same age as my older brother, who rescued Ossie from the shrubs below.
Curiously, whenever Benji's actions were questioned, his family members
responded with the same placating optimism, "that's just Benji for you."

I found Benji's behaviors confusing. He never joined me and his two brothers when we played down by the creek and around the storm drains. Instead, he would rat us out for playing where we shouldn't be. We moved to Western Australia when I was eight and my friendships with my cousins disintegrated under the distance separating us. We returned to Victoria four years later but by then the passing of time had created a chasm large enough to keep us from ever reconnecting.

My father stayed with my aunt and uncle and cousins for a few days sometime during my prepubescent years. Afterward, he recounted many stories about Benji's "creepy" behavior, like the way Benji would stalk to the curtains when he was outside smoking a cigarette and pull them aside just enough to peer out at him. He would make us laugh by playing up his uneasy reactions to Benji's unusual behaviors, callously mimicking his motor tics and slow and stalling speech. I found my father's purported uneasiness especially funny at the time because he seemed so invulnerable and frightening to me.

Benji's motor tics became a source of material for my own comedic routines, which I performed in front of family members to get a laugh. Benji was different and difference, at least to me, became something that was either funny or to be avoided. This was the least of my repulsive prejudices, however, and over time they morphed into new phobias: I refused to swim in public pools among those with visible disabilities or drink from the water fountain at school if the girl whose face was distorted with burn scars used it. Other neurotic behaviors slowly emerged: I could no longer lick lollipops because they reminded me of bald heads.

When I was fourteen my parents split up. It was an ugly separation. Weather-worn timber fences call forth memories and experiences from that time in my life; they are embroiled in a dance of significances. They remind me of my mother's white slip-on shoes and black leggings, although I can't be sure if she was wearing black leggings when she scaled the fence to escape the large kitchen paring knife my father held, or if her love of black leggings has been superimposed upon this earlier time. Other rays of the past peek through these timber fences too: I am sitting next to my father at the kitchen table in his newly furnished apartment, shortly after their separation, when he tells me in an accusatory tone that he *knows* my sister is "slow." This comes as a surprise to me. My sister is eight years younger than me. I've known about her learning disability—which, according to my mother, affects her ability to do math—since she was a kid. The word *slow* carries so much negative weight, especially the way he says it. Slow reminds me of Jobe Smith, the simple-minded gardener from the early '90s film *The Lawnmower Man*. I try and shrug off his remark, but I'm deeply unsettled because he says it like he's unearthed a shameful truth that should remain hidden.

The truth is, I'm deeply protective of my sister. I have assumed a major role in her life ever since our father walked out and distanced himself from us. We were evicted from our house after he left. My mother, me, and my younger brother and sister moved into my Nanna's cramped two-bedroom unit. He doesn't know that I read to my sister every night or stop her from crying by pantomiming the stories, ridiculously overdoing them just to make her laugh.

I would later realize that the stigma and secrecy that shrouded Benji's disability also explained why my sister's intellectual disability was never spoken about or understood in its full complexity. I'm not sure why my mother kept her intellectual differences shrouded in vagueness and ambiguity. I've since learned that there's a twenty-five-year-old cardboard box of paperwork containing the diagnostic details of her disability tucked away somewhere in my mother's wardrobe. Was my father insinuating that there was secret collusion between my mother and me, as though I were another Pandora determined to keep the lid closed on my sister's intellectual disability?

When I was in my early twenties, my partner and I worked at a children's orphanage in Blantyre, Malawi. Rooms were crammed with cribs filled with crying babies. The air was so thick and heavy with the odor of sweat and saliva that it was hard to breathe. There was a little girl who peered up at me from inside a crib and smiled, her eyes sizzling with life. Her bright and warm energy seemed to reach out and embrace me. Her name was Emma and she had cerebral palsy. I spent a lot of time with her, feeding her or just hanging out. The experience reverberated deep feelings within me and induced a feeling of shame for my past bigoted behavior. Though I had developed a perspective that was sensitive to the embodied differences among us through caring for my sister, disability still felt strangely unfamiliar to me at the time. Back then, of course, I couldn't have predicted how big a part of my life it would become—long after the last details of Emma's smiling face had wandered from my mind.

When I was thirty my first child was born. Takoda had blond hair and a deep cleft in his chin that made my Nanna cry because it reminded her of her son—who had died from encephalitis when he was just a baby, back in the 1940s. When he was four months old, Takoda started having multiple seizures a day. There were moments in the hospital's emergency department when my partner and I thought we'd lose him. By the time he was two it was apparent that he had multiple severe disabilities. I experienced a stretch of bitterness over not getting the opportunity to fulfill my imagined fatherly role. His smile reminded me of Emma's and from early on I could make him laugh the way I used to make my sister laugh. He smelled like the ocean's breeze, and his tiny body felt warm in my arms. There was something else, too, harder to explain. There had always been a void, a deep ache inside me. It had been a wellspring of discomfort, inducing feelings of homesickness in the most homely and familiar settings. Into this void rushed an understanding and love that was both resonantly familiar and unlike anything I'd ever known before.

·　·　·　·　·

In the above story I have structured my memories in a way that brings forth a sense of continuity. While it is possible for me to reflect on these past moments separately, here, they form parts of a narrativized whole. These memories and memories-within-memories have been woven together around personal significances concerning care, stigma, and disability in my life. They form inseparable parts in the dance of significances that organize my experiences of disability and fathering, giving them their depth, texture, and open-endedness. However, it is not in the act of detached recollection, that is, within a reflective and analytic attitude, that these memories have been regathered, articulated, and (re)furnished with meaning—although in some cases this is certainly possible. Rather, it feels as though these past moments have gained their own identity in the course of my caring for Takoda. These moments articulate themselves as the most durable, memorable, and significant, furnishing my ongoing experiences of fathering and disability with meaning and an inexhaustible

depth. This speaks to an implicit self-familairity that underpins our subjective experiences of selfhood across time and the way modalities of experience are always already colored by lived significances that are at once
idiosyncratic and inherited by family, culture, and history—in a way that
Heidegger would say we can never quite get behind or render completely
intelligible.[1] We can never be free of these significances or definitively
tease apart their bearing on how perceptual experience organizes itself.

There are particular moments, for example, the diagnosis moment or
telling family and friends about a child's disability, that help define the
way parents come to identify with their child's disability and their roles
as caregivers early on.[2] One of the most interesting patterns that emerged
during my research, however, was the way parents experience their child's
disability and these key moments in accordance with past experiences and
meanings. To put it another way, parents' embodied emotional histories
and incursions of memory lend form to the ways these moments and others are experienced in the first place and over time. The past plays a key
role in shaping how parents identify with their child's embodied differences, alongside motivating their commitments, structuring future possibilities, and, ultimately, helping them get a grip on everyday reality. The
role the past plays in structuring experience is illustrated in both the early
work of Heidegger and the work of Merleau-Ponty.[3] For Heidegger, we
project ourselves into the future with relation to a particular understanding of ourselves and in accordance with a past that discloses things as mattering to us in particular ways, while for Merleau-Ponty former experiences and the anticipations they engender surround our perceptions as an
atmosphere or horizon, structuring our perceptual experiences and what
articulates itself as significant.[4] To the extent that for many parents arriving to their worlds of disability often ruptures the flow of everyday experience, the past and its foreshadowed possibilities become all the more
important to understand.

EARL'S ARRIVAL STORY

Earl was twenty-five in the fall of '85 when he decided to leave the Coast
Guard, load up his Toyota truck, and head across the country for a fresh
start. After arriving in Phoenix, Arizona, he soon secured a job at the

local fire department as an engineer/paramedic and met his future wife, Suzanne, in the parking lot of a local church one morning after service. They were married almost a year later. Two years and three days from the day they met, Zachary was born.

They had planned for a natural birth. But during labor the doctors decided to perform a C-section and Suzanne was rushed to the operating room. Earl recalls sitting in the waiting room when Zachary was suddenly wheeled out of the OR in an incubator and airlifted to a neurological institute nearby.

"I'm standing there going, OK, now what?" Earl recalls. "Now what's going on? Life changed at that moment and I knew it changed. I didn't know how it changed or why it changed, but it was like life is different now."

Sitting in the doctor's office, Earl and Suzanne were told that their son had a rare neurological condition called hemimegalencephaly: one half of Zachary's brain was bigger than the other, which often causes seizures and cognitive and behavioral disabilities. The prognosis, they were advised, was grim. They were cautioned he could have uncontrollable seizures and may have to undergo a hemispherectomy, where a hemisphere of his brain would be removed or disconnected to control seizures. "We were caught completely off guard," Earl told me. "We were looking to fix our son because we didn't know what to do."

Back in 1988 there was little in terms of support and services for children like Zachary. The federal program of early intervention services for infants and toddlers with disabilities was still in its infancy, signed into law on October 8, 1986. Like other parents who are given no clear indication of disability in utero, Earl and Suzanne suddenly faced the unexpected. "We were in survival mode," Earl said.

DOUG'S ARRIVAL STORY

Doug's father was a United States Marine and so he grew up on military bases, regularly attending air shows. He joined the military himself as a young man, but the stress he suffered from a shipboard fire cut his career in the navy short. Doug was eager to share his love of air shows with his children and so when his first son, Noah, was born, that is what he did. Noah was a precocious and spritely child with a love of reading and a highly focused interest in rotating objects, like fans and wheels. The air shows were a win-win situation. They provided Doug an opportunity to continue this beloved family tradition, while permitting Noah to visually explore his love of spinning items. They spent whole days gazing at propeller blades and wheels in all their circular manifestations, amid the people, the roar of fighter jets, and the smell of cotton candy.

During an air show when Noah was two years old something unusual happened: a jet flew overhead and threw him into a horrendous panic attack. Doug managed to calm him down, but another jet soon flew overhead, inciting the same reaction as before. Doug carried his screaming son over a mile back to their parked car. In the months that followed, he began displaying strange behaviors: he started wearing sunglasses inside the house and wouldn't eat anything above room temperature. Doug and his wife, Mary, consulted clinicians and were assured he would outgrow these idiosyncrasies.

When Noah was four years old, Doug and Mary had a second child, Nick. Noah still showed no signs of outgrowing his sensory peculiarities and—perhaps more troubling still—his behavior was growing more defiant. Nick was slower than Noah to meet his developmental milestones, but otherwise seemed typical to Doug and Mary. Then he wasn't. Sometime after his first birthday he started experiencing fevers of 104°F. The doctors ran various tests, including blood tests and x-rays, and discussed hospitalization, but, ultimately, were unable to identify the cause of Nick's febrile episodes. He gradually became more withdrawn and unresponsive and slowly stopped responding to his name and making eye contact. Doug and Mary consulted a specialist about their growing concerns and another spate of tests was organized.

In the end, a speech pathologist suggested Noah had Asperger's, after witnessing his voracious appetite for books and his unusual competency with jigsaw puzzles. Within the coming months both boys were diagnosed with autism spectrum disorders.

ETHAN'S ARRIVAL STORY

Ethan and Georgina Strout married in their early thirties. Ethan was starting out his career in the toy industry at a company that manufactured and sold action figures. Georgina became pregnant with their first son, Jackson, a couple of years later. Their second son, Jack, was born in 2007. He was premature and spent three weeks in the neonatal care unit because of respiratory difficulties. But he made a full recovery and returned home, steadily reaching his developmental milestones as time wore on. It wasn't until 2009, Ethan recalled, that the trouble began. Jack experienced a mild fever after receiving his diphtheria-tetanus-pertussis vaccine—which made Ethan wonder if there might be a causal connection despite scientific evidence to the contrary—and began displaying peculiar movements known as body hiccups.

These seizures were recorded during an EEG at a children's hospital, enabling a quick assessment—so quick, in fact, that a neurologist from the hospital called Ethan and Georgina shortly after their appointment and asked them to bring Jack back in immediately for admission. Jack was diagnosed with a form of childhood epilepsy called infantile spasms. A follow-up MRI revealed they were being caused by cortical dysplasia, an abnormality in the brain's development wherein neurons fail to position themselves correctly. Ethan and Georgina started treating Jack's epilepsy with medications and watched helplessly as he slowly regressed, losing some of his speech and becoming more physically uncoordinated.

Within the next six months, the Strouts learned that a brain tumor was the focal point of Jack's seizures. At the end of 2009, Jack underwent a temporal lobectomy to remove the seizure focus. "Nothing really prepares you for seeing your nineteen-month-old kid lying on a bed, pale-skinned and barely moving," Ethan recalled. Eventually, Jack received an autism spectrum diagnosis: pervasive developmental delay, not otherwise specified (PDD-NOS).[5] This string of events, Ethan said, was "a symbol of when life changed for all of us, a point from which there has been no turning back."

. . . . .

The arrival stories depicted above describe profound moments of disruption that move parents toward experiential disequilibrium. For many parents, their experience of a ruptured world lifts the veil on what was thought to be familiar and determinable, throwing light on taken-for-granted assumptions and the habits and routines of day-to-day life. A sense of continuity and predictability are displaced by a perceived mismatch between the present and a past that was supposed to lead somewhere else. The above arrival stories illustrate the profound disjuncture parents face between a lived past and where it was supposed to lead and their new situations as caregivers. Scot, who cared for his severely disabled daughter until her death at the age of twenty-seven, lamented: "It's like a unique new agenda for families, situations that we're in. They didn't really exist before. It is so overwhelming. Your life is completely turned upside down and absolutely readjusted in a way that—it affects everything you do, all your ambitions."

The new agenda that Scot describes refers to the cultural and social shift toward community care in the context of post-deinstitutionalization in North America. Thirty-odd years ago it was common for parents to relinquish their severely disabled children to institutions, often upon the advice of specialists. This is perhaps an unsettling thought for some and difficult for many parents to fathom today, in an era when informal and family caregivers have come to play a key role in the care of their disabled children.

The protracted and emotionally tiring nature of caring for children with severe disabilities demands a strength and determination that are not easy to sustain. A recent study found that caregivers involved in providing complex care are more likely to experience emotional, physical, and financial difficulty than those providing less substantial care, are 5.3 times as likely to experience participation restrictions in valued activities, and are 3 times as likely to experience work productivity loss.[6] Of the fathers I spent time with, all their children were still living at home under their care and vigilance.

In her essay "A Different Light: Examining Impairment through Parent Narratives of Childhood Disability," medical sociologist Susan E. Kelly suggests that parents of disabled children achieve normalization by undergoing a "conscious re-embodiment of the social category of parent."[7] This process also has a tacit dimension that does not involve such deliberate and reflective modes of reembodiment. There is something to be said about past moments that are invisibly present in parents' embodied experiences of disability and caregiving.

Past moments can haunt the edges of experience, that is to say, they are intuitively perceived even before they have been deliberately evoked or consciously reflected upon. In the case of the fathers in this study, the past gives their experiences of disability and upheaval their particular experiential quality of being unique. In some instances, of course, it is possible that the tension toward equilibrium may remain unresolved until explicit reflection and/or narrativization helps determine the matter. But other times, experiences of disruption have an experiential character from the outset or tacitly assume one over time correlative to past moments and what they afford in their remaking. In the words of Marcel Proust, "each new character is merely a metamorphosis from something earlier."[8]

LIVED TIME

I am sitting in the living room of Earl's beige two-story home in suburban Scottsdale, Arizona. He peers at the clock; he is waiting for Zachary, his twenty-seven-year-old son, to arrive home from his day program. When Zach's bus finally arrives out front, Earl rushes outside to greet him. Moments later, Zach comes inside with Earl. He is dressed in a blue T-shirt and shorts. There's an awkward glide to his gait, a spring in his step that is encumbered by his inward turning toes. He opens a plastic bag and hands Earl a football fan-towel he purchased earlier from his favorite sporting store with the help of his home heath aide. Then he makes a beeline for the sofa and begins shedding his shirt and shoes—an evening ritual I have heard Earl describe numerous times. He plonks himself down and points a lazy finger toward the television. "Thomas," he mumbles.

"'I don't want to watch Thomas," Earl says, feigning boredom.

Zachary flaps his hands, grinning. "Choo, choo."

Moments later, Zachary leads me and his parents up a winding staircase to his bedroom on the second floor. The room is elegantly furnished with rich brown oak. A flat-screen TV is mounted on the wall in front of his bed, and there are shelves and storage baskets along the walls filled with toys and children's television shows on DVD and VHS. There are posters scattered across the wall behind his bed: Bear and the Big Blue House, Barney, Kermit the Frog, the Muppets, Sponge Bob, a football poster.

Every night, Earl tells me, Zachary sits on the floor and creates a collage with his favorite toys while watching TV. As foretold, Zachary kneels on the floor, his chest bare and his legs curled under him, and begins spreading his toys out before him. Earl helps him choose his favorite ones from a stack of storage cubes against the wall.

Earlier that day, Earl described his struggle with his grief in the aftermath of finding out that Zachary was disabled. He drifted away from his family and escaped into taking "care of the things men do," he said, namely, breadwinning—while Suzanne provided Zachary with full-time hands-on personal care. His feelings of estrangement were grounded in the disappointment and grief he felt over realizing that his long-held dreams and expectations were irremediably lost. "I'd never been down this road of having a child with a disability," he recalled. "I was planning on having a boy, playing catch, and all of a sudden I found myself with a child that's nonverbal, he's always going to live with us, he's incontinent, and we're always going to be changing diapers."

As they spread toys across the floor together, I marveled at the communicative bond he shared with Zachary and struggled to imagine the chasm he had described ever existing between them. Of course, Earl couldn't have known it at the time of our conversation, but in two years' time Zachary would transition into a community residence and he and Suzanne would take their first overseas trip together.

Earl described his emotional return to his family as an "evolutionary process." Slowly disability became the center of his life's work. Fifteen years after Zach's birth, he decided to create a men's support group in Arizona for fathers of children diagnosed with disabilities. He said that he wanted to create a space that fostered support, learning, mentorship, and a sense of community for men who were struggling with the same unchartered waters he had faced alone over a decade earlier. He was also acting as chairman of the Arizona Developmental Disabilities Planning Council when we met, in addition to his work with the Scottsdale Fire Department delivering emergency preparedness training for persons with developmental disabilities and their families. During the summer of 2015, Earl and I attended an emergency preparedness summit together in Phoenix, where he was an invited guest speaker. During his address, he disclosed that his life as Zachary's caregiver and involvement in emergency preparedness work were founded on his earlier experiences caring for his father as a child.

In 1969 Earl Sr. dropped a friend off at the hospital and was headed down Route I-5 in Portland, Oregon, when an intoxicated driver, heading down the wrong side of the interstate, collided with him. At age twenty-nine, Earl Sr. became a quadriplegic. Earl recalled visiting his father in the hospital and seeing him strapped to a circular bed with a tracheostomy tube for ventilation. "You're now the man of the household," his father said to him, "take care of your mom and your sisters for me." "From that moment on," Earl said, "my childhood was over." He quickly assumed his place as "man of the house" and all the manual tasks and responsibilities that came with it. "I think that's why I love fixing things. It's always been a part of who I am," he said to me.

One afternoon in Scottsdale, we were sitting in the courtyard at the rear of his favorite pizzeria, the sun slicing down on us, when he reiterated that his past had prepared him for his life as a caregiver today.

"It's like you're a piece of clay and God's sculpting you," he said gently.

I knew that Earl believed in some kind of divine order to life, but I was more interested in hearing about his past experiences that enabled him to reconfigure his world and transform his self-understanding.

"How has He sculpted you?" I asked.

He told me that for a long time he felt angry and bitter that he was robbed of a childhood. "He [his father] required a standard of care that stopped us from doing regular everyday things that families do," he said, recalling how he used to help his father move about the city streets—in the days before electric wheelchairs—and the negative reactions Earl Sr.'s disability elicited from those within the community.

"People would stare," he said. "They'd be like, who's this twelve-year-old kid pushing this six-foot man around in a wheelchair? I remember he couldn't get into certain stores because the wheelchair wouldn't fit or there were stairs." Despite these attitudinal and environmental barriers, though, Earl said his father maintained a positive attitude and even started his own support group for the mobility impaired at a hospital outside of Portland.

"He taught me perspective and how to embrace life," Earl recalled with an easy self-confidence.

Then he segued into a story about his uncle who had lost both his arms in a logging accident. During his childhood, Earl recalled frequently visiting to assist him with bathing and cleaning up. At the time, he said, home life was beset with problems. His mother was struggling to come to terms with her husband's accident and so her drinking escalated. She had reached an advanced stage of alcoholism by the time of Earl's adolescence, fueling his desire to leave home.

"She was a role model of what not to do," he said, smiling bitterly. "I remember coming home from high school and she would be passed out on the couch, you know, smoking cigarettes. And my dad would be in bed, whistling and hollering because he couldn't do anything for himself. It destroyed her life and the peripheral people around it." Then, in a moment of consolidation, Earl said, "Growing up in Oregon, my dad's accident, choosing to help care for my uncle who was a double amputee, all the fire service activity that has connected me to a diverse population of people, these things helped prepare me for Zachary. So, it's been compounding over the years with all the stuff that has happened and then culminating with Zachary." He breathed a sigh of relief. "It's like there's a reason for all of this. God has a plan."

TEMPORAL SHIFTINGS

Writing about the productive way individuals make sense of their memories, psychologists Steven D. Brown and Paula Reavey describe the functional approaches that have been taken toward understanding autobiographical memory.[9] Citing the work of psychologist Martin Conway, they discuss the role episodic memories play in increasing our perceived orderliness of the world, wherein those memories most relevant to our current goals are more likely to be drawn upon in offering the most value.[10] "Autobiographical memory," they write, "is the reshuffling of past experience to create an orderly present and coherent life trajectory—or 'long-term-self'—where what we are doing now appears entirely congruent with what we have done before."[11] This active element involved in remembering was captured by earlier thinkers like Sigmund Freud, who argued that the material present in the form of memory traces is "subjected from time to time to a *rearrangement* in accordance with fresh circumstances—to a *retranscription*."[12] This perspective is quite different from that of those who posit memory in purely mentalistic terms, that is, detached from the surrounding world and occurring within the confines of the head, as representations or engrams.

The way Earl consolidates his memories can certainly be seen to create a connection between past events and his life as Zachary's caregiver. However, it is the ways past moments are refurnished with meaning through his ongoing experiences that offer the greatest insights into the "evolutionary process" that saw him reconnect with his family. As anthropologist Tamara Kohn writes, "We think and feel through memories, and, as we travel through time around the world, the memories grow with us."[13] Our pasts and futures are in a perpetual state of becoming. They are refurnished with meaning and are newly articulated in relation to the interplay of shifting contexts and changing identities that accompany our experiences over time.

Merleau-Ponty uses the term *la chair* (the flesh) to describe the indissoluble link between body and world.[14] According to him, the body and world are not ontologically separate but born in mutual relation. The body is made of the same flesh as the world. "They are in a relation of... overlapping," he writes.[15] In *The Visible and the Invisible*, he introduces the related idea of "reversibility" to describe the reciprocal and reversible exchanges between one's flesh and the flesh of the world in perception.[16] Using the example of one hand touching the other, he illustrates the body as both perceiver and perceived, object and subject, sensed and sentient.[17] Embodied acts of caregiving involve shifts between feeling and being felt, touching and being touched, perceiving and being perceived. I will discuss this further in the next chapter when I consider embodied care and bodily resonance. What is relevant here, however, is how Merleau-Ponty characterizes time in the same fashion: "The past and present are Ineinander," or being-in-one-another, "each enveloping-enveloped."[18]

The tensioned shifts that occur through caregiving, between feeling and being felt, seeing and being seen, invoke past moments and transform their meanings, and, in doing so, inform how parents understand present events, the stories they situate themselves in, and the futures they press into. What is remembered and anticipated articulates the foregrounded meanings of the now, which in turn refigure memories and possible futures. Earl's childhood experiences with his father's disability and the neglect brought on by his mother's alcoholism contextualized my understanding of why he estranged himself from his family early on after Zachary's diagnosis. But his capacity to make sense of his life as a caregiver is contingent upon the very same past, its depths and the potentiality it affords in its (re)making.

One morning, we were sitting in the late morning sun as it poured through the windows of his living room. He said, "Having a child with a disability really impacts how you respond because they're different. You have to find a new type of value because your life is never going to be like it was. It took years before I was able to really start identifying how I felt about Zachary. How did he feel about me? And I think that was the big thing, knowing that Zachary loved me, that Zachary wanted to be with me." I recalled Earl's words from an earlier time, from that day we had lunch in the bright, leaf-dappled shade in the pizzeria's courtyard, when he told me that his father taught him to appreciate the simple things in life, "a gentle look," he had said, "a touch. They're very important things."

Many years passed between Earl's early experiences of bewilderment and grief after Zachary's diagnosis and the time it took for him to acquire a "new value system." And yet, a part of his story attests to his having acquired a perspective sensitive to the contingencies of life and differences among people early on, through his childhood experiences of caring for his father and the lessons his father taught him. Here, his past combines with the present, illustrating the perpetual becoming of time and the constant movement of existence, our self-understanding as "an unfolding into a future which is enfolded in a past, itself unfolding into a future."[19]

Earl stared at me, conviction washing over his face. "When Suzanne was pregnant with Zachary, I put my hand on her stomach and said, Lord, fill our child with your wisdom, your way, not the worlds. That he may know you uniquely. That this child be blessed by you. Well, if I pray that prayer and all of a sudden I'm given a child with hemimegalencephaly and the doctors are going, we've never really seen this before, I got to believe in God's answer to prayer."

Here, the past returns to itself anew, "electrified with the charge of later connections."[20] Earl understands himself and his life in accordance with these temporal movements backward and forward. Importantly, these temporal shiftings hold possibilities for maintaining a sense of self-continuity across time and recreating an understanding of one's life in accordance with the necessities of the present and the anticipations it foreshadows. In the words of Merleau-Ponty, the past is found in an "openness upon general configurations or constellations, rays of the past and rays of the world at the end of which, through many 'memory screens' dotted with lacunae and with the imaginary, pulsate some almost sensible structures, some individual memories."[21]

THE PRESENCE OF THE PAST

Doug remembers sitting with Mary in the speech pathologist's office, listening to her describe potential autistic behaviors. The boys hadn't been diagnosed yet. Doug found every trait the speech pathologist described resonating with him strongly. "Everything she kept identifying," he said, "I was just going, that's me. I'm like that. I was like that. I do that. I did that."

Doug has never been officially diagnosed with autism. But in the eight years since his boys were diagnosed, he says that everything he has learned constantly reaffirms his conviction that he is also on the spectrum. Doug nods his head in acknowledgment of how disorienting it must have been for Mary to find out, within a matter of six weeks, that the three men in her life had autism. He chuckles and admits that he couldn't stop thinking at the time, "This is the greatest thing I have ever learned."

On a warm July evening in Tempe, Arizona, Doug and I are sitting in his kitchen-dining room when he leans forward in his chair, staring at me, his eyes iridescent with a mixture of peace and sorrow. "It explained my whole life," he tells me. "I was almost thirty-eight years old, and I had lived in this deep dark void in space not understanding humans. It was devastating for their mom. But for me it was an opportunity to help my kids because I directly understood portions of what they were going through." Doug recalls becoming a valuable source of insight for Mary into the boys' atypical behavior. "Mary realized that I could relate so much to what she was reading, so she would ask me, do you think the boys think like that? Do you think like that?" Shortly after his sons' diagnoses, Doug joined a group for adults with Asperger's. "The more I learned about it the more I came to understand myself," he says. It suddenly made sense to him why he has been obsessed with numbers all his life. The more he thinks about it, he admits, the more he is convinced that his mother is also on the spectrum.

Months after our first meeting, I am sitting in his living room on a weathered brown three-seated couch next to his eldest son, Noah. Noah looks a lot like his younger brother, Nick, but pubescence has thinned him out. Nick is sitting at the table where I sat back in July, eating a bowl of chips, humming to himself loudly and making sounds that aren't quite words. It's Halloween. In the kitchen, Doug is on the telephone, finalizing sleepover plans for Noah. Eight photographs hang on the wall to my right—Nick and Noah are pictured in each one—above a small three-tiered bookshelf filled with self-help books with titles like *The Art of Connecting* and *The Courage to Be Rich*. The living room serves many purposes. There is a desk pressed tightly against a wall, papers scatter its surface and spill over onto the floor. There's a cream-colored lateral filing cabinet next to the desk, rows of bulging manila folders arranged on top. The crowded space reminds me of Doug and the balance he seems to have achieved between chaos and order in his life.

My eyes fall on a large lithograph hanging on the wall above the filing cabinet: a dilapidated barn amid wide open grasslands, presumably somewhere in the Midwest. When Doug rejoins us in the living room, I tell him I like the picture. He gives me a perky smile and tells me that, with the right lighting, the sky above the barn looks like watching the sun rise and sun set at the same time.

"I was in the Navy, in Russian language school in Monterey, California," he says, staring at the picture, "and my buddy and I were walking along downtown Monterey and, I don't even know why I went in there, we were just kids—"

"Damn kids," Noah interjects.

"We were like twenty-one years old," Doug continues, undeterred by Noah's interruption, "and I remember just walking down the street and there was this—"

"You're a spy," Noah shouts.

Doug giggles. "I was supposed to be," he says to Noah. "Anyway, there was this gallery and we walked in and I stopped in my tracks and that [the picture] was like looking in the mirror. I was looking in the mirror. And that was back before I understood any of this [the boys], and, like I said, I don't have a diagnosis but, you know, clearly, I'm like my kids."

"What was it about the picture?" I ask.

"It was like, wow! There's this entity that's isolated. It's very solemn. It's very quiet. It's very meek. Like I said, I spent the first thirty-eight years in this deep dark void in space and I looked at that thing and it was like looking at a picture of me."

Nick begins pacing back and forth, from the dining room to the living room. His splotchy green T-shirt clings to his rounded body. He claps his hands and makes indistinct noises as he passes us on his well-trodden circuit. There's a singsong quality to his exclamations, like he's doing vocal warm-up exercises. Then, in a quiet and polite voice he asks his father, "Go outside, please."

Doug peers at him over his glasses. "You want to go outside?"

"Outside," Nick confirms.

Doug lets Nick out through the sliding glass doors at the rear of the living room that open onto a small veranda where a mammoth green cocoon-swing hangs from a beam in the ceiling. Nick nestles into his cocoon and begins slowly swinging around in circles. As we watch Nick's circles gain momentum, I ask Doug if he feels the same when he looks at the picture now as he did all those years ago as a young man in Monterey.

"Oh yeah," he admits. "My perspective on a lot of things has changed with the understanding of autism. I moved around so much as a kid that we never recognized that I always had really weird social patterns. I have very few friends that go past a couple of years. It's still a pattern that I have yet to break. I don't have those deep roots around me. I think that has a lot to do with it."

For Doug, the confusion surrounding Noah and Nick's atypical behaviors lifted quite suddenly that day in the speech pathologist's office. Like a snap of recognition, his past experiences of estrangement and isolation reminded him of his present situation as a father of two boys with autism. The moment of a child's diagnosis is often described by parents as a catalytic event that creates deep change, demarcating space and time into before and after. Doug's past experiences of isolation and loneliness invoked a sense of familiarity in the face of the boys' diagnoses, disclosing a new understanding of himself and facilitating a new understanding of and connection to them. In viewing Nick's and Noah's autistic identities as inherited, Doug has established a genealogical connection to his boys, a connection that has kept feelings of estrangement at bay.

Doug's recognition of autism and self-discovery is not an act of intellectual synthesis in which life events are reflected upon and merged with the present for clarity and order. Rather, memories and past significances help determine how he finds himself attuned to a world that experientially matters in particular ways and the perspective he adopts toward his children, others, and the situation as a whole. As Gail Weiss notes, memories are one of many perceptual phenomena not part of the sensory field at any given moment that are operative in the significance found in a particular situation.[22] The past hangs in the background of perceptual experience as a horizon against which a situation arises into affective prominence, is understood, and is responded to.

A focus on attunement throws light on the dynamic and wavering way the world is disclosed and experienced by fathers in relation to their personal histories. Attunement implies a dynamic figure-ground (object-horizon) structure of perception that arranges the world into meaningful gestalts. The ground, or horizon, against which a figure or object reveals itself, while unthematized and indeterminate in the sense that it is not being explicitly attended to, plays an inseparable role in how the presentation of the object is experienced. For example, as Merleau-Ponty observes, the lighting in the room plays an indeterminate normative role in how the color being attended to is experienced.[23] The figure-ground structure is a totality and reflects a temporal and spatial organization correlative with one's attention, interests, experiences, and expectations. As phenomenological thinker Jennifer Bullington expresses it, "foreground and background only exist between a subject who meets a view with certain interests and attention, and a world that shows itself in terms of the subject's interests and attention."[24] The "world outside isn't imprinted upon us like a photograph, she writes, but is "taken up in an active moment of meaning constitution."[25]

For Doug, the mist of uncertainty around his boys' diagnoses and behaviors dissipates through recourse to past experience and an amorphous subjective feeling of being alone and different from others that has plagued him from childhood. Through his mode of being attuned to the world and interactions with his sons he has begun reflecting on these past moments more thoroughly, which has triggered a process of profound self-revelation.

PAST HAUNTINGS

I first met Ethan outside the doors of the Hilton Garden Inn on a warm summer's evening in Columbus, Ohio. We had arranged to have dinner upon my arrival. It was close to 7 p.m., and I had worked up an appetite over the course of my eight-hour transit to the Midwest from Arizona. My first image of Ethan was a rear view: peering out across the empty parking lot and over the road at a steak house where a hundred or so biker enthusiasts had gathered for an expo. He was wearing a Baltimore Ravens baseball cap, shorts, and a black polo with bold white letters sprawled across the back and spelling *Nintendo*. He sensed my presence as I exited the doors, and turned to face me. His face was bordered by a ginger gray–colored goatee and black-framed glasses, behind which peered out a pair of blue inquisitive eyes. He looked different to how I imagined him. This is a weird claim to make of someone I had never met before, but Ethan didn't feel like a stranger to me. I already knew partial bits of his life as a caregiver for his autistic son, because I was a reader of his online blog. I guess he didn't match the image that accompanied my readings of him.

He was a lot quieter than I had anticipated, soft-spoken and pensive, bordering on broody. His attire spoke to his previous job as vice president of creative development at a toy company that had since gone defunct and to his laid-back approach to entrepreneurship: he spent twenty-minutes in the parking lot of a Japanese restaurant that evening outlining his ideas for a handbag designed specifically for men—with all its masculine cosmetic trimmings—demonstrating its capabilities with a pseudo-prototype he brought to dinner.

Despite the simplicity of his attire, there was a melancholic depth that revealed itself, at least at first, in subtle ways: in a momentary pause mid-sentence or in the silences that bookended his eloquent verbal renderings of particular experiences. Over time, Ethan would reveal himself to be not only introspective but acutely self-critical. He seemed to be on a quest to remake himself in the face of the challenges encountered through his lifestyle as a caregiver and the intensified moral responsibilities he felt.

"I believe there's something about people who have suffered trauma where there's a connectivity between them," Ethan said, staring at me astutely one afternoon as we sat in the living room of his house, which overlooked a quiet suburban street lined with elm trees. He was referring to our pasts and shared experience of domestic violence, alluding to how these traumatic experiences become anchored at great depths within people, reverberating across time. When Ethan was five years old, his biological father left home and severed ties with his family. By the next year, when Ethan was six, his mother had remarried, to an overbearing and quick-tempered man whom he describes as a white-haired force of nature. His stepfather, whom he alternately refers to as his father, condemned him to a violent childhood that slowly started to chip away at his self-esteem. Outwardly sophisticated and seemingly charming, backstage he was a cruel man who began subjecting Ethan to physical and psychological abuse. The cruelty stretched on for over a decade and culminated in a violent confrontation between them one afternoon when he was sixteen. The confrontation came as a surprise to his mother, he recalled, who had not been aware of the abuse he had endured over the years. "He was always good at keeping her in the dark," Ethan said. He recalled some of his stepfather's more mundane terrorizing tactics, like waiting for him to return home at night by hiding in a corner of the dark house and then unexpectedly leaping out to slam him against the wall, shoving his hand into his throat to pin him there. "That is creepy dark shit to do to a kid," Ethan said. "It does something to your brain." Many years later, his stepfather killed himself with a .357 Magnum.

Ethan got up and moved in front of the window, his attention divided between the quiet street and talking to me. "Any sharp or sudden veers or anything like that don't sit well with me," he confessed. "Physical punching and pinching make me extremely upset," he continued. "I get closed off and tight and reserved. It affects me. I take medication for it." He paused, reflecting. "It's a role reversal. Instead of father to son it's son to father. As a kid I was powerless against my father and then I regained my power when I left and started to find my own voice and life. And then Jack came and took that power away from me. He assumed my father's place and there are times when he has complete power over me, just like my dad did. It's this creepy twist of life. I am not completely at peace with that yet."

I told Ethan that my son cycles in his moods and behavior, from being irritable and agitated one week to calm and at ease the next. "Jack cycles too," he said. "He's in a good cycle at the moment but when he comes out of that cycle he will hit more and, like I said, when he does the pushing or pinching or emotional rejection, I struggle more. Those feelings, post-traumatic stress, I feel that more and start to say, did I ever get away from him?" He paused again, letting the thought linger in the air. "But the difference is I want to be with Jack. It was easier with my dad, just leave and say I'm done, I'm finished. This is a whole different thing."

The body can be seen here as a horizon that continues to mediate how Ethan experiences the world and caregiving. Traumatic past moments go on living in a general style of existence, manifest in the ways in which he experiences Jack's physical assaults and perceived emotional rejections.[26] Perhaps the biggest challenge Ethan faces is remaking the present in light of the past's unflagging bodily persistence and intercorporeal presence.

Traumatic body memories are past experiences that leave indelible marks on our subjectivity by anchoring themselves in our bodies. Philosopher Edward Casey writes, "Body memory alludes to memory that is intrinsic to the body, to its own ways of remembering: how we remember in and by and through the body."[27] More broadly, body memory refer to the ways well-practiced motion sequences and other repetitive patterns of perception and interaction become embodied as knowledge or skills in our daily practices.[28] This includes our history of primary experiences with others, which is expressed in our emotional and behavioral dispositions and implicitly shapes our relationships with people.[29] Implicit memories take on an absent presence by subtending conscious life as one of many habitual horizons that orient us in time and space. Implicit memories are, as Fuchs writes, "based on the habitual structure of the lived body which connects us to the surrounding world through its operative intentionality."[30] Thus, the perceived world is invested with meanings and values correlative to bodies and lives.

In the preface to *Phenomenology of Perception*, Merleau-Ponty describes

the distinction phenomenologist Edmund Husserl makes between intentionality of act and operative intentionality.[31] The intentionality of act is
the level of intentionality associated with conscious acts, such as judgements and "occasions when we voluntarily take up a position."[32] Operative
intentionality, on the other hand, "produces the natural and ante-predica-
tive unity of the world and of our life, being apparent in our desires, our
evaluations and in the landscape we see."[33] For Merleau-Ponty, operative
intentionality is the condition of the former's possibility and the thread
that ties us to a world where things have significance and solicit actions
from us. Unlike the kind of habitual body memory that ensures spontaneous and reflexive skillful action needed for free movement and dealing
with situations, Casey highlights how traumatic body memories have the
potential to constrict such efficacy because the trauma disrupts spontaneous actions.[34]

Our histories of embodied interaction, therefore, continue to exert an
influence over the way we relate to and interact with the world and others. Jack's displays of aggressive behavior pose serious challenges to the
ways Ethan is able to understand himself and his situation. Memories of
domestic violence, written into the very way he exists in the world, bear
down on his lived experience. While for some the depths and potentiality of the past allow for the emergence of new aspects of self-making and
discovery, traumatic past moments taken up by the memory of the body
impede Ethan's rediscovery of the past and ability to make new connections with it.

NARRATIVE HORIZONS

Stories have long been recognized as an important element in finding
order and meaning in our lives. Anthropologist Cheryl Mattingly writes
that "we locate ourselves in unfolding stories that inform our commitments about what is possible and desirable . . . about how things should
and will unfold."[35] While lived experience is always more complicated
than narratives can delineate, they are one of many cultural resources that
assist individuals in reorienting their lives, a way of "redrawing maps and
finding new destinations," as sociologist Arthur Frank phrases it.[36] "To

think with a story," Frank writes, "is to experience it affecting one's own life and to find in that effect a certain truth in one's life."[37]

All my participants located themselves within unfolding stories. Many of them find resonance with Frank's three narrative types—restitution, chaos, and quest storylines.[38] Simply put, restitution narratives are couched in modernist expectations that there is a remedy for every illness. They focus on the restoration of health. According to Frank, this is the preferred narrative in our contemporary culture of restitution. Chaos narratives, on the other hand, are the antithesis to modernist restitution narratives. They imagine life never getting better. They are hard to bear witness to, he says, because they lack any discernible order or causality and therefore induce anxiety in the listener.[39] They are more of an "anti-narrative of time without sequence," he writes.[40] Typically, in telling our stories, events are mediated by the telling; however, in lived chaos "there is no mediation, only immediacy."[41] Therefore, chaos stories cannot really be told, according to Frank, but are only ever really lived. The third narrative type Frank identifies is the quest narrative, which is characterized by movement. The protagonist in these stories is active and undergoes some form of transformation through the illness experience, becoming a dyadic body in their desire to reach others and make a difference in the unfolding of their stories.[42]

Frank's narrative typology is useful in discerning certain thematic threads that run through fathers' stories and the work these stories do for those telling and receiving them. Some of the fathers I spent time with showed a great affinity for quest stories. Both Doug and Earl, for instance, invoke the notion of a transformative journey and frequently speak of acquired insights that they want to share with others to help them. For others, however, the past makes the hardships of the present uncomfortably intolerable.

Ethan frequently spoke of the pain in his body, "mental, physical, and emotional." He said, "I just do what I can and accept being in agony every day." Another time he lamented, "A dense fog prevents me from seeing but a short distance ahead." Ethan's experience exemplifies a chaos narrative, wherein he is ensnared in a what can be described as a web of immediacies and chaotic moments. According to Ethan, Jack's behavioral problems contribute to his anxiety and depression, stirring up old trauma and perhaps stifling the potentiality of movement found in quest narratives. If stories provide a medium for patterning our memories into narrative order, keeping "the body out of chaos," as Frank puts it, then traumatic body memories can keep one living the chaos, standing like roadblocks to our narrative paths.[43] Returing to the figure-ground structure of perception, attention is selective and able to shift or reverse the figure and ground. Weiss suggests that when the figure-ground structure become too fixed, pathologies can arise.[44]

I witnessed Ethan fight against the insistence of his traumatic past, describing the immense pride he feels when he sees his oldest son displaying patience beyond his years with Jack, despite their tumultuous relationship, or moments of revelation when he appreciates all the amazing things in his life. There were times I observed him placing his experiences within the broader genre of a transformative journey: advising fathers to consider "the measurement of the wonders your child is to you, not who your child isn't."

Then, his narrative would be disrupted, and he would admit to the difficulty of arriving at a definitive account of his experience: "That whole positive thing I tried? I wanted it. I could taste it. But I couldn't maintain it. . . . My life just isn't that and has never been that. And from the look of things, it will never be that. I can't false project an air of total positivity and feel that I am being honest. It feels like wearing someone else's skin. That doesn't mean I want to be negative either. I just can't lock myself in to any one thing."[45]

TEMPORALITY AND SELF-REMAKING

To explore the grounds of possibility for the way people experience their worlds and articulate new permutations of meaning requires considering the biographical significances we bring to bear in the ongoing project of creating our lives in a common field of experience with others. For many of the parents in this book, the depths of the past and its potentiality afford creative developments and new forms of self-understanding and recognition that affect the ways they relate to the world, while others find their best efforts at making new connections to themselves and their history of experiences thwarted by the past's unflagging presence. My focus on the various ways fathers are attuned to the world throws into relief how particular situations are anchored in other situations, and how the possibilities we get ourselves into facilitate the passage from one situation to the next, a sense of rupture, or a new course of action.

What is clear is that memories play a primary role in what the juncture between the future and the past affords in its making. The past is vital to bringing strangeness into familiarity and sustaining a subject's sense of existential continuity across time and after disruption. Thus, the histories that we carry with us not only disclose things as experientially mattering in particular ways but also provide important grounds upon which we understand ourselves, make new meanings, and press ahead into new possibilities. Memories are deeply personal and interpersonally significant. They are a necessary part of the background that situate parents' experiences of care and important grounds from which to understand their indeterminate and changing perspectives.

Gary's Arrival Story

It was Good Friday, April 2003, and Gary had the week off from teaching. He'd just finished visiting his wife at work in Phoenix and was on his way to the mall with their seven-and-a-half-month-old daughter, Mia. Gary took the off-ramp and came to an abrupt stop behind a line of cars. Red lights flashed ahead, signalling that structure work was underway. Behind them, the driver of a flatbed truck was distracted because he had dropped a road map under his seat. He was still fishing about for the misplaced map when he turned onto the off-ramp. Gary recalls seeing the truck barrelling down on him and Mia. By the time the driver realized that traffic had come to a stop closer to the freeway than he had anticipated it was already too late. The onrushing truck slammed Gary's stationary car from behind at sixty miles an hour, spinning it forward two hundred feet. Gary's seat collapsed into the back seat and the windows burst, showering glass everywhere.

When Gary gained awareness, he realized Mia was unresponsive and covered in glass. He started screaming her name. Passersby attempted to calm him, but it was no use. He feared the worst: Mia was dead. Then, Mia let out a few small grunts.

There were no fatalities that day. Gary's scapula was broken and the passenger in the tow truck sustained a broken leg. But Mia spent the next five weeks in the hospital. During that time, she underwent surgery for a subdural hematoma (bleeding between the brain and skull). Gary and his wife, Cherry, were cautioned that Mia might not survive. But she did. After ten days in the ICU, Mia was transferred to the local children's hospital, where she was treated for more internal swelling. Family flew in from Pennsylvania but there was nothing that anybody could do. Gary and Cherry were preoccupied with Mia's recovery, and the ordeal had consumed their thoughts and spirits. At the end of May Mia returned home and started her new life of therapies.

Over the last twelve years Mia has made developmental strides, but her acquired brain injury caused multiple physical and cognitive impairments that will require care for the rest of her life.

3 Between Bodies

THE FLESHY WORK OF CAREGIVING

Every day around this time they navigate the early evening streets together. They are a most unusual sight: big and small, old and young, hobbling through the urban landscape between townhouses and along uneven streets. For familiar others this sight must border on the banal— after all, Paul has lived here with Pearl for over twenty years. He has been her sole caregiver since she was baby. He bends his tall body over Pearl's wheelchair, bearing his weight down through the handles to propel her body forward. Every now and then she moves her head from side to side and flashes a wild and unbridled smile. Words he said to me earlier linger with me, reanimated with new significance as I accompany them in their dyadic solitude: "She is absolutely a part of me. We have a very strange connection. I can walk into her room because I know she is seizing without having heard anything. So, we have a connection on various levels."

We arrive back at their place—one of the only single-story homes in the area— as the light lowers in the sky and casts long shadows that run away from us. Paul points to a large Japanese cherry blossom tree standing in the front yard. Its thick knotted trunk supports a network of gnarly branches that seemingly bend under the weightless clusters of fleecy pink blossoms.

"I planted that tree a year before Pearl was born," he tells me. He regards the overgrown and unkempt lawn that surrounds and stretches beyond the tree's elegance. Affecting an air of defeat, he says, "I have pretty much ignored my yard and let it overgrow like crazy because I just don't know what to do with it."

He heads back inside with Pearl. I stay a bit longer before the tree, which has stood strong and steadfast over the years, while love and beauty have grown and youth and vigor have passed in their wake.

· · · · ·

Time and time again, I heard men recount intimate caregiving routines that are the stuff of everyday life. Beyond affirming their sense of value as fathers, these accounts of their hands-on, tactile experiences of care—as told to me and in the various versions I heard them tell familiar others—were often pervaded by an intense emotionality. With remarkable synchrony, the fathers I spent time with often remarked that what seems insurmountable in the beginning is slowly "embraced" through time. When I pushed them to elaborate on how they think caregivers achieve this existential reorientation, they invariably defaulted to particular moments of touching and proximity with their children, moments that spoke to the transmission of unarticulable meanings.

The moments of shared intimacy between fathers and their children that I describe in this chapter invite us to think about the corporeal and affective grounds upon which care is enacted by and for others. They bring to light the centrality of the body and its capacity for resonance and fellow feeling as the basis of ethical life and the key to making care possible. These interactions highlight the body's affective powers in awakening a deep resonance with otherness and embodied resonance as a vital medium for learning and moral change.

In *A Child Called Noah*, Josh Greenfeld documents day-to-day life raising a child with autism.[1] He observes with discouragement, "His is a world I am shut out from, mine is a world he has been unable to enter."[2] Greenfield's description is consistent with the commonly held view that autism leads to interpersonal incompetence, even intersubjective impenetrability. Similarly, those with severe intellectual disabilities are thought to be born with limited interpersonal capacity. In this sense, the inner life of individuals cannot be possibly known or entered by another. Thus, the inevitable question arises: how do we gain access to the minds of others in the context of profound difference? There is however, a counterstory that broadens our understanding about forms of intimacy and gestures toward bodily reciprocity and the relational space between bodies. In this story, parents gain certain kinds of access to the inner lives of their children in the absence of verbal or cognitive communication (sign language). The stories in this chapter speak to a world in which there is an interdependence between self and other, where tactile and interaffective experiences enable caregivers to assimilate a real, if incomplete, understanding of how their children experience the world. A relational understanding of the body helps bring to light how parents recognize the mental life of their children through embodied experiences of caregiving.

THE BODY AS A VEHICLE FOR CARE

A midsummer heatwave rolled over Phoenix, and the East Valley broiled in daily temperatures above 109°F, matching records set back in 1896. It was 10 a.m. and we were seated around a table outside IHOP. I poured myself a hot coffee and silently scolded myself for my stupidity. At this time of the year the bustling metropolis slowed to a lethargic crawl, a stark contrast to the cooler months when snowbirds, fleeing their bitter winters, seek solace in these same streets and strip malls. It seemed all but IHOP's most loyal patrons had surrendered to the pitiless sun, moving to inside seating. I knew why we were outside. I employed the same strategies when dining with my son in public. Outside provides respite from the echo and incessant boisterous commotion unfolding between the restaurant's walls—a sensory nightmare for some. When there is no outside seating available, my son enjoys being squashed underneath the table, which breaks all types of cultural rules governing public behavior and never fails to elicit righteous and confused looks from strangers or misguided comments from family members. I don't care! Not anymore, at least. The darkened space beneath the table provides him solace from the multisensory spectacle that fills him with such unease.

I was the youngest father at the table by at least ten years. Gary, a retired teacher in his forties, sat next to me, his hands folded over his rotund belly. Earl sat across from us with Zachary, who was thoroughly immersed in a *Thomas the Tank Engine* video playing on an iPad resting on the table. Charles, a man in his sixties sporting a full head of thick gray hair, sat a few chairs down from Zachary. Everyone at the table knew everybody else, except me. We ordered breakfast and Earl glanced around expectantly.

"There's supposed to be more guys coming," he said.

Gary shoots him a confused look in response. It's clear to me that Gary isn't sure whom else Earl could be expecting. I wondered if Earl was feeling anxious about the size of the group, given that I'd traveled all the way from Australia with an explicit interest in fathers' attendance at his support meetings. True, it wasn't much of a turnout, but I had anticipated this. Gary had informed me a week earlier that the meetings often churn out the same faces—a group of men who have known each other for many years, going back to when Earl first started running the meetings some ten years earlier. It had been a while since they had recruited a fresh face, at least at this chapter, anyway—Earl organized several other meetings across the Valley during the month, which I was looking forward to attending.

Over the next hour conversation ranged far and wide: beard oil, the financial crisis, travel, internet usage, the heat wave, race relations in America and the Charleston church shooting in South Carolina—Gary gives Earl a lesson on racism and the "white power structure." To my surprise, no one talks about their children. No one talks about disability. It is mentioned only once and that is in relation to the church shootings and discriminated groups. Was this because the men were all so well-known to each other? Was I yet to realize how mundane caregiving became over time? Or did the presence of someone new pose barriers to more intimate exchanges?

During these conversations, Earl feeds Zachary a plate of pancakes. There's a rhythm to the feeding; a joint awareness to the activity, even though neither Earl nor Zachary are attending to it explicitly. Zachary chews and swallows the forkful of pancakes he has been given and then opens his mouth for more. Earl scoops pancake pieces onto the fork and brings it back up to Zachary's mouth. Zachary doesn't have to wait with his mouth hanging open, signalling for more, because each anticipates the other's movement. It's a dance of finely tuned readings. Sometimes Earl brushes excess food off Zachary's lip before it falls, or anticipates spillages before they occur. This is carried on as background activity to the main event, which is, for Earl, the conversation about white privilege: Earl is intensely engaged in a dialogue with Gary.

I sit back and remain silent on the topic of conversation, despite my views regarding the structural and everyday injustices perpetrated by white supremacy. I am cautious about expressing my opinion before I have built a rapport with anyone, lest I be excluded from further participation. But I am also enthralled by the feeding, the subordinate activity Earl is involved in. A smile bursts across Zachary's face as he watches *Thomas*, and Earl stretches a hand behind his shoulders and gently caresses them.

· · · · ·

The scene at IHOP typifies the ways the "body masters a novel skill by incorporating its own corporeal history of hours and days spent in practice."[3] For instance, Earl's movements while feeding Zachary are not calculated, rather intuition guides them. Also, this repertoire is thoroughly interactive, as its successful accomplishment hinges upon Zachary's reciprocal ability to read Earl's movements. Earl illustrates several habitual abilities that are backgrounded during the feeding, including a feel for the fork and finely tuned discriminations concerning how much food to put on the utensil and the best angle to deliver it into Zachary's mouth. Earl's movements are responsive to a host of contingencies, which include Zachary's postural changes and gradations in mouth movement. It is unlikely Earl remembers the feeding or that he has ever deliberately reflected upon its jointly achieved operation.

This example offers one illustration of the ways in which certain things, like fine motor movements, recede into the background of our perceptual awareness in order to sustain our attention to the task at hand. As discussed earlier, this thematization is crucial to the ways Merleau-Ponty understands the orientational structure of the phenomenal field. Most notably, Hamington has taken up the theme of perceptual disappearance in his work on embodied care to suggest the body is built for care.[4] In an eloquent passage, Hamington describes the tactile nature of washing his daughter's hair and the ways he consciously attends to her while the fine motor skills that accomplish the task and the sensory data that constitute his tactile perception are absent from direct perceptual focus.[5] He suggests that the body's disappearance from perception thematizes the world in such a way as to make care possible.[6] In other words, a primary condition for enacting care is engrossment in the other, which requires self-effacement.

Whether it be through routine feeding, scaffolding motor tasks and learning experiences, or holding and comforting a child through a seizure, the demands of caregiving call parents into different styles of being; that is, through new skills and competencies parents' bodies are reorganized and refigured in ways that allow for new forms of agency. Merleau-Ponty's use of the body schema concept is important to my argument here for several reasons. I begin here with a bit of definition, in order to understand the emergence of new potentials that arise through caregiving.

In his magnum opus, *Phenomenology of Perception*, Merleau-Ponty argues that the experiencing subject's orientation in space and apprehension of the world is directed by what has become embodied knowledge through the lived body's daily engagement in physical situations.[7] The *body schema*, as he understands it, connects the lived body to a world with meaning and potentiality through the body's situational understanding of space and spatial features. For Merleau-Ponty, the body's active engagement with the world is the center of all perceptual experience and consciousness. Central to his phenomenological account of the body is his concept of *motor intentionality*.[8] "Grasping an object," philosopher Sean Dorrance Kelly says, "is a canonical motor-intentional activity."[9] According to Kelly, this kind of intentionality cannot be explained in terms of the spatial understanding that informs reflective or intellectual acts, like pointing at the doorknob to identify it, for example.[10] Skillful actions like typing on a keyboard or the kind of understanding you have of a doorknob when you unreflectively reach out to open it display the kind of unreflective understanding that is characteristic of this form of bodily intentionality. As such, two vistas spread before us: things present to conscious thought (explicit knowledge) and those things we apprehend or "grasp" via our motor intentionality. In contrast to a disembodied Cartesian consciousness, for Merleau-Ponty, consciousness is not a matter of "I think that" but of "I can" (respond to the world).[11] Our primary relationship to the world, then, is one of practical skill.

For Merleau-Ponty, the acquisition of skill and knowledge changes our relationship to the world by determining the boundary conditions that specify what shows up as meaningful and our arena of possible actions. In other words, the more we learn from our experiences, the more our experience feeds back into the way the world is experienced and the possibilities we see for acting.[12] He calls this the *intentional arc*, which "projects round about us our past, our future, our human setting, our physical, ideological and moral situation, or rather which results in our being situated in all these respects."[13] Philosopher Hubert Dreyfus describes Merleau-Ponty's intentional arc as a feedback structure: "The agent immediately sees things from some perspective and sees them as affording a certain action . . . Skills are stored, not as representations in the mind, but as more and more refined dispositions to respond to the solicitations of more and more refined perceptions of the current situation."[14] For example, if a parent has to rush a child to the hospital because they are very sick or are having a seizure, then the acts of leaving the house, starting the car, driving in the direction of the hospital, negotiating traffic, watching traffic signals, parking, and so on are elicited without calculation. The necessary movements to perform the task are implicitly given and establish the pathway between here and yonder. Thus, the experiencing subject is oriented in space and apprehends a world that solicits engagement through movement, learning, and practice.

Perception and embodied skill are integrated at the level of the body schema, which, as I have already mentioned, accounts for our pre-reflective grasp on the world and the ways we are set to deal with a situation.[15] The body schema is a system of motor-sensory capacities that function without the necessity of perceptual monitoring.[16] It operates according to the latent knowledge the body has of the world. Therefore, it is at the level of the body schema that the meaningful world is composed and articulated. In the language of Merleau-Ponty, the acquisition of new skills or the appropriation of new instruments that are incorporated into "the bulk of our own body" changes existence by refiguring the body schema.[17]

New skills and capacities, then, can be said to dilate our being-in-the-world. The most often-cited example is the blind man's cane, which,

Merleau-Ponty argues, ceases to be an object open to synthesis in its use and instead extends the scope of the skillful user's motility and bodily consciousness.[18] In carrying out our intentions, therefore, our embodiment is extended through the incorporation of objects and tools that facilitate our actions. If I'm in the habit of driving, to use another of Merleau-Ponty's examples, the car becomes an extended sense of my body, whereby I can feel where it begins and ends without any deliberation about its size and volume as an object in space.[19] Importantly, these body-schematic performances are not explicitly owned, because over time they become habitual, sedimented bodily skills, knowledge that becomes part of the embodied self and disappears from conscious awareness.

Through regular repetition new caring skills are incorporated into the body schema and extend the body's repertoire of action-related possibilities. This bodily plasticity enables parents to respond in increasingly sophisticated ways to their children and carry out their own daily tasks and roles as caregivers. However, these skills are not sufficient conditions alone to motivate parents to endure the difficulties they face as caregivers or account for the sacrifices they make in raising their children. To understand this, we need to appreciate the conditions of passivity and of being touched that are an equally important aspect of our being-in-the-world; an aspect of experience that offers possibilities for parents' perceptual remaking and becoming.

BETWEEN BODIES

Doug has the air conditioner cranked up all the way, blowing frigid air around the kitchen. We are sitting at his kitchen table. The rest of the house is dark and quiet, except for a lamp in the living room that casts softs beams of light across the floor. There's a weighty melancholic atmosphere in the house; an eerie contrast to the weekends, when the boys are around infusing the space with an energetic lightness. Doug looks tired. Dark circles encase his eyes. He tells me that, between working odd jobs and dealing with Nick's behavioral problems, he feels "pretty drained." A couple of months back there was an incident at school, in which Nick bit one of the teachers six times. "The bites were so bad it took eight weeks for the bruising to go away," he recalls. The following day Nick also gave his mother her worst bite to date and uncharacteristically started physically lashing out at his two-year-old half brother.

"Before we could get a response from the doctor we went ahead and reduced the medication back to the level it was a couple of weeks prior and immediately he started getting better," Doug says, shaking his head. "But that was months ago and he's still not back to where he was." His lips tighten into a half smile as he tells me that they've been in "crisis mode" the last few months, "trying to get additional behavior supports."

After their divorce, Mary and Doug's solidarity over the welfare of their children remained intact. They continue to work together to provide the most supportive and loving atmosphere for their boys, a fact Doug is proud to talk about. "I think the divorce rate is in excess of eighty percent with special needs kids . . . But we never lost sight of our kids," a situation, he says, that is not lost on therapists and case managers who often compliment them on their united effort ensuring the boys get the support and care they deserve. Doug admits he had been unaware that there were so many couples who were driven apart by their child's disability and their own conflicting interests.

Many of the parents I came to know during fieldwork reported the same statistic concerning divorce rates in families with disabled children. Some of the sources I found estimate that up to 85 and 90 percent of marriages disintegrate because of the stress disabled children bring to families.[20] However, writing about the history of autism in *NeuroTribes*, Steve Silberman calls this statistic a "pernicious myth" perpetuated by the media, noting that families with children who are disabled are in fact at no higher risk of divorce.[21]

"I hear it is dads who leave because they can't deal with their kids," Doug shrugs. "I don't understand that."

A few years ago, Doug hurt his back, which stopped him from being able to carry out many of his most cherished routines with the boys—like bathing Nick. Because Nick is hyposensitive, he enjoys the sensory input from the water at bath time. Doug describes the quiet moment they would ritually share together at night before his injury, as he pulled Nick from the bath, wrapped him in a towel, and nursed him in his arms. These days, Nick is too big to be nursed and has graduated from bathtubs to showers.

In the shadowy quietness of the kitchen, Doug says, "My new thing is, I sit on the edge of the toilet and he just buries himself into my chest, puts his head on my shoulder, and if his arms are on the outside of the towel he hugs me and . . ." Tears cloud his eyes, as he goes on, "That's my favorite moment with him because he is at his greatest peace of any time—he's smiling, he's laughing, he's playing in the mirror, he's engaged with me, face-to-face, eye-to- eye." Doug wipes the stray tears that have escaped down his face and continues, "His world is just so chaotic beyond that. It's probably the only time he hugs that hard."

.   .   .   .   .

For Merleau-Ponty, the experiential connection between self and other is present from the outset of our lives, allowing bodies to extend and connect to one another. In his late conception of "the flesh," touch becomes his primary example of perception. Flesh is an experience of contact, not distance. The flesh encompasses the space between caregivers and those they care for and speaks to the coexistence and cocreation of self and other, "the coiling over of the visible upon the seeing body," in Merleau-Ponty's words, "of the tangible upon the touching body."[22] Merleau-Ponty's idea of *reversibility* describes the reciprocal and reversible exchanges between perception and the flesh of the world being perceived. Using the example of one hand touching the other, he illustrates the body as both perceiver and perceived, object and subject, sensed and sentient.[23] These mediums cross over and are intertwined. Each experience makes the other possible.

As philosopher Kym Maclaren tells us, "The true living hand, when it is touched, feels to the touching hand as if it has a life within it, a nascent intentionality, such that it could turn itself back on the touching hand; and in turn, the touching hand feels in itself its own latent intentionality."[24] She argues that it is not the case that the touching hand has the potential for being touched and vice versa, for this introduces too strong a separation between these two terms.[25] Rather, there is a genuine ambiguity, "an activity that is also a passivity, and a passivity that is also an activity."[26] Through the medium of the flesh we are constantly open to the world and others, continually mediating between touching and being touched, affecting and being affected, self and other. This relational ontology, the idea that our relationships constitute our reality and who we are, provides the grounds for interpersonal communication and attunement, whereby two people can align emotionally and behaviorally to achieve understanding.

My feet are fastened to Takoda's in a pair of joining sandals. I stand and adjust the tension in the straps so that our bodies are positioned correctly and are in alignment. I look down at our bodies coupled by a web of material, Velcro, and plastic. It is a strange sight for me to see him stand so upright. I wonder how tall he is in comparison to his peers. I take a step and his leg follows mine. I can feel his hesitation and the weight of his leg through my own, so I wait for him to initiate the next step. He does. My leg follows his through space. Slowly, we find a rhythm and begin moving as one. I must deliberately alter the length of my stride but otherwise we achieve synchronization. There are reversibilities at play. At times I lead. At others I trail. I am both passive and active. I am mover and moved. Sometimes we move in unison and it's hard to differentiate. We kick a soccer ball: I swing our legs and our feet make contact with the ball, which hurtles across the room. "Hey," I beam. He squeals and looks up at me. His face is awash with joy and his eyes are full.

Through the intertwining of our bodies a shared space is brought into being, "of which neither of us is the creator."[27] Within this shared space a sense of emotional symmetry emerges, wherein my radiance affects my son and his joy affects me, an emotional experience that is cocreated and attributable to neither of us in isolation. An emotional intimacy and a sense of his agency are enriched through our joint negotiation of movement and space. In the beginning, I can feel his hesitation to follow my lead and so I wait until he initiates the next step. He does. I can read my gesture in his movements as he begins moving toward the soccer ball. Similarly, my body grasps the significance of his volitional powers through his movements, as can be seen by my waiting for him to initiate the next step after his initial moment of resistance. I can feel myself oscillating between leading and following until we attune to each other's movements and synchronization is achieved.

An intimate space for communion is actualized through the lived body's capacity for symbolic communication and affectability. We understand each other through bodily reciprocity. Moments of affective intimacy between parents and their children can be thought of as moments of meeting, located somewhere between touching and being touched. When communication is achieved, it "is as if the other person's intention inhabited my body and mine his," writes Merleau-Ponty.[28]

There is an inherent ambiguity in this notion of reversible intertwining, namely, how our coexistence with embodied others is ambiguously both encroachment and differentiation. That is to say, it is by virtue of our social existence and primordial openness to others that difference is experienced or conceivable at all. Philosopher Rosalyn Diprose writes, "It is through this ambiguity of bodily existence that new possibilities for existing are open to me."[29] She explains: "Whether learning a new skill or inheriting someone else's kidney, my possibilities are borrowed from the bodies of others, always with an incalculable remainder."[30] The chiasmatic relations to which Merleau-Ponty refers are always "imminent and never realized in fact."[31] Therefore, while a truly absolute other does not exist because bodies extend into and encroach upon one another, they never collapse into sameness. The relational other retains their singularity. Recognition of this fact is important because responsive and empathetic care requires responding to the uniqueness of the other.

SENSORIALITY

Care ethicist Nel Noddings describes engrossment as a feeling with the other toward whom we move.[32] She characterizes engrossment as an open receptivity to the person being cared for and a genuine regard for their needs, desires, and well-being.[33] Motivational displacement in her words is essential in ethical caring, where a transfer of "interest from my own reality to the reality of the other" occurs, motivating the one caring to act on behalf of the other's interest.[34] But how do parents involved in the care of their severely disabled children achieve the level of engrossment and responsivity necessary in caring for them? How do they take on their child's reality as a possibility for the self and develop the receptivity necessary for enhancing "the power and activity of another"?[35] Or expressed differently, how do parents access the life and mind of their children in the absence of language and cognitive communication (gestures and sign language)? The reversibilities at play in caregiving offer insights into tactile and affective experiences that can deeply impact our existential and affective sense of being.

Through caregiving for my son, I have become more aware of the ways the senses open us onto a world thick with meaning and comprise a bodily perspective from which the world articulates itself. Merleau-Ponty's view on synesthetic perception is apposite here.[36] In writing about synesthetic perception, he refers to the body as a "synergic system" that provides a holistic experience of the world through unification of the senses. The senses blend together and are united in our apprehension of the world: "I hear the hardness and unevenness of cobbles in the rattle of a carriage," he writes, "and we speak appropriately of a 'soft,' 'dull,' or 'sharp' sound."[37] As Heidegger puts it, we hear the creaking wagon and not "noises and complexes of sounds."[38]

This synesthetic ability is fundamental to our experience of the world. And yet sight has been privileged through Western intellectual history because it has been central to the production of scientific knowledge, giving vision its privileged status as a way of knowing in modern Western cultures. The other senses have thus been relegated to an inferior status, denigrated as inferior modes of knowing the world in which we breathe. Ocular-centrism, therefore, can be seen as a historical and cultural trap that, in the words of Merleau-Ponty, "shifts the centre of gravity of experience, so that we have unlearned how to see, hear, and . . . feel."[39] Overprivileging our sense of sight has consequences for how we orient ourselves in space and time and how we relate to others. It could be said to lead us to superficial understandings of the world by casting our attention to the surface of things.

Strangers often judge Takoda according to what they can see. He can't handle crowded public spaces. Their dynamic sounds and motion send him into a panic. Strangers might see a boy writhing and wiggling, hands clasped tightly over his ears, screaming and grimacing as he attempts in vain to overcome his sensory surroundings and restore some equilibrium. Internationally renowned autism self-advocate Temple Grandin likens her sensitivity to loud noises to the pain one might feel when a dentist's drill hits a nerve.[40] "High-pitched continuous noises such as bathroom vent fans or hair dryers are annoying," she writes, and "certain frequencies cannot be shut out."[41] One child told me that listening to his mother sing produced the sensation of pins prickling his flesh from the inside.

Beach visits offer a vastly different sensory experience for Takoda. He will sit contentedly on the sandy shore as small waves break over his legs. I feel as though he would be quite happy to sit there the entire day, gently paddling the shallow surf with his hands and squeaking intermittently, in what is an expression of unbridled and immense joy. The wide-open space, the sun's warmth, the cool water, and the gentle hum of the rolling surf provide him with solace and calm, a place to be. Here are some other things he likes: water play, cold foods and soft, smooth textures, spinning objects, gliding his hands through corn kernels and feeling them sift between his fingers, my singing gently into his ear, positive touching, his sisters piling on top of him, mom tickling his back with her cold fingers, smiling along to his favorite song, Bob Schneider's "Mudhouse." Through acting as a caregiver to my son, I have come to realize that ruptures in reciprocity and understanding between people are not only the result of neurological and social disjunctures but also involve bodies and physical environs. Not all spaces are created equal and while there are many that he can project into easily, there are many more that restrict his modes of embodiment.

Visual and textual biases pervade parents' worlds of disability: from the detached stares of strangers invoked by their children's embodied differences; the diagnostic labels and definitions that are used to describe the specificities of bodies; the numerous charts and evaluative measures that professionals use to assess the capabilities of children so that parents can access supports and services. These biases trigger the objectification of their children, overlooking what we already know deep down: the full sensorium is intimately involved in the ways we evaluate, discriminate, orient, and communicate with others in everyday situations.

In the attachment theory literature, reciprocal patterns of interaction are said to aid in the development of infant-caregiver attachment formation. Among men in Ireland, for instance, masculinities scholar Niall Hanlon identifies reciprocal emotional benefits as motivation for providing care, such as experiencing emotional intimacy and feeling loved.[42] But as Andrew Solomon asks in *Far From the Tree*, "What becomes of the transaction with an MSD [multiple severe disability] child, who can often express only appetite or pain, then signal satisfaction when hunger and discomfort are assuaged?"[43] Understanding embodied interaction between caregivers and their severely disabled children in the ongoing cocreation of their worlds is a good start.

Being with and feeling with Takoda has helped me shed some of my cultural domestication by opening me to other ways of knowing the world, rooted in the reversibility of the flesh and embodied sensorimotor experiences; a world that is grasped and composed through the body across the senses. In the presence of each other and through our shared history of interaction, Takoda and I often fall into a space of attunement. The bodies potential for coupling enables a partial and pre-reflective grasp of the ways he emotionally relates to and is affected by the interiority of spaces and their atmospheric qualities. And this is not a superfluous matter! Beyond having a forceful impact on his emotions, these sensory spaces motivate certain behaviors and influence the ways he emotionally perceives and responds to future situations.

ATTUNEMENT AND INTERBODILY RESONANCE

Through taking care of Takoda and feeling with him the resonance of my feeling body has been altered and refined to a workable degree of interbodily resonance. I now quite instinctively grasp the atmospheric qualities of certain spaces and how he relates to them. Atmospheric sensitivity is described by architect Juhani Pallasmaa as an "unconscious and unfocused peripheral perception," which he defines as a biologically derived emotive capacity to instinctively capture the atmospheres and moods that are overarching qualities of our environments and spaces.[44] Fellow feeling bridges the gap between parents and their children and affords responsive caring actions.

We enter a restaurant, moving into the space; the unanimous voice of its already seated patrons is muffled by the soft furnishings and fabric-covered wall panels. There are no sounds coming from the kitchen. The arrangement of the furniture and the various partitions break up sound paths. The audibility of the space feels welcoming; the sounds spread and resound evenly. There is adequate spacing between the tables, which lightens the density of the room. We walk toward a booth situated at the back of the restaurant; the air is infused with the soft aromas of rosemary. The dim lighting, warm color scheme, and the symmetrical and minimal arrangement of artwork hanging on the walls create a restful and calming effect. All these elements pull together to create a pleasurable spatial experience for Takoda. I resonate with him. There is consonance between our bodies, selves, and the world that prevents any conceptual reduction to isolated selves. A buoyant feeling arises as my muscles relax, my breathing deepens, and I energetically dilate into space. It's a delicate balancing act.

In moments like these the boundaries between my body and Takoda's become less defined, engendering profound moments of experiential connection and understanding. Atmospheric effects (sounds, smells, colors, sights, illumination, layout, rhythm, motion) pervade our embodied experiences more generally, and my son's quite intensely. Our capacity for preverbal communication is crucial to making sure he is cared for properly and that his embodiedness is respected. Bodily resonance is grounds for communion and the development of embodied relating.

Building on Merleau-Ponty's concept of intercorporeality, Fuchs emphasizes bodily resonance as the basis of social understanding.[45] He writes that, through our history of interactions, "social understanding and empathy develop as a practical sense, a musicality for the rhythms, dynamics, and patterns of interactions with others."[46] His conception of bodily resonance suggests that we are attuned to others in nonconceptual ways, before objective apprehension. Similarly, philosopher Anya Daly suggests our histories of interaction with the world and others affectively inform the body schema, contributing to the structure of experience and behavior. By virtue of our body schema the somatosensory cortex plays a key role orienting us in time-space via our "motor-sensory GPS," as she puts it; at the same time, we are oriented in intersubjective space by our "affective GPS."[47] Returning to Merleau-Ponty's notion of the intentional arc, if affect and emotion also inform and orient our attention and interactions with others, then affective and tactile engagements offer an important medium for moral change. Through iterative acts of caregiving and registers of meaningful engagement with their children, parents are drawn into different forms of awareness that can open new possibilities for perceiving, acting, and relating to others.

．　．　．　．

In Columbus, Ohio, Ethan is playing with Jack in the living room. Out-side, the sky is darkening. Jack is in his pyjamas. He throws a large green plastic ball to Ethan. I am watching their game from an old armchair in the corner of the room. Georgina is sitting on the floor next to me, cross-legged. She tells me about a new parent support group she has joined and how she expects its focus will be on sharing information with other parents about disability support and services. She quickly redirects her attention to Jack and applauds whenever he catches the ball. I follow suit. Jack beams with excitement and also claps, shouting, "Yeah!"

"Good job, buddy," Ethan says.

"Good job, butty," Jack repeats, still beaming.

"Did you just hit a home run?"

"Yeah," Jack smiles. "Again. Catch," he demands.

"Yes, sir." Ethan throws the ball back to Jack and he catches it again. Everyone applauds. A clear intimacy shapes their interaction. There is a rhythm to their play, like a dance, just as Ethan described to me earlier.

Earlier in the week, we were driving northward along the highway, heading back to his house. Ethan had just finished giving me a tour of the neighborhood where they had lived a couple of years ago, prior to fore-closure. We sat in the car across the road from their former, two-story house, which is nestled away in an upscale neighborhood among other colonial-style homes with green manicured lawns. Ethan was deep inside himself, caught up somewhere beyond the bay windows flanking the front of his former home, captured by the memories embraced within, memo-ries transfigured by time, always in motion. The experience left him in a reflective mode. As the scenery transitioned from houses back to farm-land, he told me that most of his interactions with Jack "are like a dance."

"It's a ritual type deal," he tells me in his characteristic careful and soft-spoken voice. "I used to think *Rain Man* was a bunch of Hollywood shit," he confesses, "but it's actually not. There's a lot of truth to that movie because if you start talking to Jack and he starts answering a couple of questions, you think he can talk to you. But he can't. If you say, Jack, did you have a good day today? Yes! He'll always say that. That's the answer he gives every time. No question. Whether he had a crap day or not. A lot of our conversations are just for the benefit of doing it. I don't know how to describe it. It's an emotional thing that I think he likes. He reacts well to it. There's a rhythm or cadence to it. Like the other day we were throwing the ball to each other, and he was getting frustrated because I wasn't doing it right. He was looking at my face to react a certain way and then he sat down. I was doing it wrong; I think. So, I just sat down. It's weird."

According to the psychologist Richard Erskine, "Attunement is a kinaesthetic and emotional sensing of others—knowing their rhythm, affect, and experience by metaphysically being in their skin, and going beyond empathy to create a two-person experience of unbroken feeling connectedness by providing a . . . resonating response."[48] Importantly, though, while this feeling toward the other with whom we move has the potential to enhance the quality of caregiving, attuning is a mutual process; that is to say, communicative power is shared. Parents and their children move through varying degrees of convergence and distance according to the level of shared bodily resonance and understanding between them at any particular time, as the scene between Ethan and Jack illustrates.

In their study on communication in caregiver–care receiver dyads, Colin Griffiths and Martine Smith examine the ways reciprocal feedback loops regulate how each person in the dyad engages with the world and with the other in the interaction process.[49] They suggest that dyadic attuning varies along two interfacing continua, one representing empathy (mutual understanding) and the other cooperation (in pursuit of a common purpose).[50] Thus, attuning can be asymmetrical; for example, "one partner may be highly . . . 'attuned' to another, while the latter may demonstrate far less empathy, to the point of ignoring the partner or refusing to cooperate."[51]

During moments of reciprocal and symmetrical attunement there is harmony between me and Takoda; a rhythmic attunement characterized by emotional, bodily, and cognitive synchronicity. In these moments, he may smile or laugh in seemingly shared amusement. He may make momentary eye contact. He is receptive to being affectionately caressed and touched. Correspondingly, I feel a sense of expansion and openness. I feel lulled, confident, and happy. In these moments, I find myself taking the shape of a competent and caring father. Contrast these to moments of misattunement, wherein he screams and withdraws from me and I find myself constricting in space. I feel challenged, tense, and uncomfortable. In these moments, I find myself feeling imperfect and, at times, incompetent.

Fuchs and Koch refer to this phenomenon as "interaffectivity," or "interbodily resonance," where "our body is affected by the other's expression, and we experience the kinetics and intensity of his emotions through our own bodily kinaesthesia and sensation."[52] This circular interplay of expressions and impressions modifies each partner's bodily state, as "they have become parts of a dynamic and sensorimotor and interaffective system that connects both bodies in *interbodily resonance*."[53] Through these shared affective states parents and their children converge emotionally. In cases where children lack verbal communication, interbodily resonance provides grounds not only for communication between bodies but also for the development of affective connections between parents and their disabled children that cognitivist theories fail to account for.

As can be seen in the examples above, there is no absolute fusion between self and other. Our capacity for resonance does not presuppose harmony; on the contrary, touch can be experienced as transgressive or alienating—as I discussed in the last chapter in relation to Ethan's history of physical abuse and how this has shaped his lived space, or in the case of many people with autism who can be quite averse to touching. The resonance of the feeling body—patterned by our histories of embodied socialization and interactive experiences—the emotional perceptions these resonances influence, and a person's corresponding action readiness play a foundational role in structuring the phenomenal field and our interpersonal relations and experiences. Within the context of caregiving, the ways caregivers are existentially and affectively oriented influences their capacity for responsiveness and attunement.

These important mediums of engagement unveil the important ways children act upon their parents. The body's capacity for inter-attunement is a form of empathy constitutive of subjectivity/intersubjectivity.[54] The experiential connection between self and other can be strengthened through bodily proximity, embodied communication, and developing caring skills and habits of attention that dilate our sense of relatedness to others. By developing these caring skills and habits parents become attuned in new ways to the everyday situations they move through with their children. This is key to more effective and responsive caring action.

INTERCORPOREAL INTIMACY

For many caregivers, their understandings of their children arise in the lived space between them, which raises the question of the conditions of the emergence of these inter-relational spaces fostering the development of attunement and care. Intercorporeal forms of intimacy between the fathers and children described in this book shed some light on how these spaces are prepared and brought into existence.

It was the last day of my first stay with Paul and Pearl in Massachusetts. We were having lunch inside the Dumpling House restaurant in Harvard Square. Over a plate of steaming wontons, he tells me, "It's very easy for me to see things through her eyes. I look at her and I get it. The environment, even physically, I can see things through her eyes." When I ask what he attributes this sense of togetherness to, he responds, "Just hanging out with her. We would both be watching the TV, or I'd tickle her, just sitting around physically, that's how we would relax in the evening. I can't do that anymore, she got bigger and is too heavy. Every night I would hold her before going to bed and talk to her and sing her songs that I can still sing and instantly get a reaction. Just made up songs. There was a mockingbird song," a reminiscent smile breaks across his face, "hush little Pearl don't you cry, Daddy's gonna buy you a pizza pie . . ."

Back at their place, Paul engages in his nightly routine of catching up on email and other work-related issues. Pearl sits in her wheelchair to his side, gently stroking the keys of the toy piano sitting on her wheelchair tray. To Paul's right, a flat-screen TV peeps out from the same giant wall unit housing the computer he works from. The unit is a disorderly site, filled and stacked to capacity. Amid the plenitude there seems little of value beyond the sentimental. A couch sits against the opposite wall. It is in a similar state of disorder, blanketed with objects. In the back corner of the cramped, multipurpose space there is a large mobile changing bench and a small screen for privacy. There are photos hanging on the wall of Paul and Pearl and their life together. The muffled sounds of the television and clicking keys unfold against a pregnant background of silence. Paul stares at the computer screen and although his attention is anchored in the synthetic world before him, his hand caresses Pearl's. At times, his hand shifts its contact to her leg, at other times he perches her foot onto his knee.

Paul frequently berates himself for not talking to Pearl more often. He tells me that she has no means of effectively communicating her thoughts or feelings. "How long would you talk to your kid without any feedback whatsoever?" he asks. "A week? Twenty-two years?" He laments feeling guilty over not talking to her more: "I don't talk to her. I can't talk *with* her." Paul feels this as a moral failing, because "parents are expected to talk to their children." Yet, despite the silence that enfolds them, Paul recognizes that they share an experiential connection. Throughout my time with them, I noticed they were frequently in physical contact with one another. Below the threshold of these conceptual understandings of how parents are "supposed" to interact with their children there is a more primordial form of communication at play between their bodies. Intimate, personal knowledge of one's child and their lived social experience is taken in by the fullness of the sensing body, through caressing, feeling, and touch. Interactive patterns that afford rhythmic communication and the synchronization of reciprocal movements are established and can stabilize into habits of care that afford close attunement and trust. These mediums of transmission are crucial for the development of corporeal connection shared by parents and children.

During fathers' support meetings and other public engagements, Earl often espoused the importance of "rebuilding your life" and finding "new hope," "new dreams," and a "new type of value system." On many occasions he repeated, "Your life can be richer and deeper because of your child's disability if you allow it to." When I asked him for concrete examples of how one actually goes about achieving such an existential and moral reorientation, Earl invariably defaulted to particular interactions with Zachary: "My son, he is twenty-six. Cognitively, he is like a two-year-old. This morning I came home from the fire station, I went to his bedroom, he wasn't awake yet, and he sits up and looks at me with a huge smile on his face and he goes, 'aaiieeee.' And I lay at the end of his bed and he turns and drops his head into my left shoulder and rolls back and forth, going 'aaiieeee,' and I'm like, if that's not love, what is?" Earl didn't elaborate beyond the specificities of the moment. It was as though he assumed everybody he told these stories to would grasp their significance.

These intimate moments embedded in caregiving routines do more than nurture the space between parents and their children. They bring about profound moments of connection, sacred moments of meeting that cannot be willed or uncovered directly. This notion of meeting is related to the body precisely because iterative acts of care can reform the boundary conditions of perception and action, opening the possibility for new kinds of engagement, moving us to make ourselves anew. Importantly, these moments are tied to the difficult aspects of parents' existential situations; they live together with and make possible the moments of reciprocity that unfold in the relationship between caregiver and cared for. These moments of meeting are sites of emergence, that is, places of imaginative and transformational potential.

MORAL IDENTITIES AND IMAGINATIVE HORIZONS

In speaking of how fathers' everyday patterns of interaction and encounters with their children contribute to a background sense of being-in-the-world, I am claiming that the fathers in this book develop an intuitive awareness and understanding of their children's feelings and intentions through embodied interaction that affects their understanding of the world. This is crucial to meeting a child's needs in an attentive and responsive way. Through habits, skills, and embodied relational knowledge, the body is drawn into certain possibilities for acting and relating to others. Experiences between parents and children mediated through bodily resonance can bring about a new focus and understanding of the world and one's pursuits, that is, of what matters most. Because the knowing subject stands embodied, the knowledge enacted through potential actions is inexorably connected to identity formation. As Hamington puts it, we cannot disentangle political and moral actions from what we know and who we are.[55] He suggests our stock of caring embodied know-how, when combined with propositional knowledge, has the potential to breed clearer imaginative possibilities for the ways we relate to those outside our sphere of experience,[56] as seen by parents who link their personal advocacy agenda to the lives of those touched by similar issues. For example, Paul's style of being-in-the-world and pursuits have changed throughout his twenty-odd years of caring for Pearl. Through his work as a special education advocate, he is currently concerned with opening up spaces for change within educational and social milieus that don't extend, protect, and accommodate people like his daughter. Returning to Merleau-Ponty's idea of the intentional arc, we can see how experiences of care feed back into caregivers' worldly concerns and moral identities as caregivers.

4 Conditions of Possibility

FATHERING, MASCULINITY,
AND MORAL (RE)ORIENTATIONS

We are standing in the kitchen of Ethan's single-story, weatherboard home. He is making coffee and telling me how much he likes his mother's partner, George: "He's a *really* nice guy. I remember being at their place once and they were installing a washer and dryer and he wanted to know if I wanted to help him. So, I did," he pauses a moment and makes eye contact with me, his mouth hanging open in thoughtful appraisal, and continues, "During the process of doing that I broke down in tears and he asked me what was wrong, and it was because the whole experience of helping him do that was so different than when my father would ask me to help him. When my father asked me to help him it was give me this. Grab this tool. Put that away. Shut the fuck up! Get out of my way. It was just a horrible experience, till eventually he might just clock me with one of the tools. I mean, that's why I have such an aversion to tools."

Ethan's story brings me back to myself and awakens my past. I'm twenty years old. I'm sitting at a small table in the kitchen of a two-bedroom farmhouse that my father purchased and remodelled a couple years after the divorce. It's a small structure —white clapboard siding and a metal roof—set amid fourteen acres in a rural town outside of Ballarat in Victoria. It's miles from anywhere. My father is standing by the stove cooking from a recipe he recently learned from his mother, eyes fixed on Gus through the window—a black Rottweiler he claims he bought to protect the property (and not to assuage his isolation and loneliness). The dog is cautiously exploring the edges of a large dam, set against a backdrop of shadowy pine trees. I listen to him boast about his nephews (my cousins), whom he recently caught up with and who both work in trades. He's brimming with unsurprising satisfaction at their transition from boys to "men's men" who work with their hands.

"I'm going to have to show you how to do a few things," he tells me, "so you don't end up a useless male. You don't want to be a useless male?" But it's not really a question and there's no sense of irony in the way he says it. He doesn't look at me, and I'm relieved, because I can feel the effect of his words in my breathing. One glance in my direction would surely undermine my uneasy attempt at nonchalance. I keep quiet. It's late and I'm not in the mood to be driving home. The last time I confronted him—over a homophobic tirade, many years before my brother would reveal that he liked the bodies of men—he stood before me trembling, barely containing his violent impulses. "Sparks are going to fly," he warned me, wagging a thick calloused finger in my direction. His uncontrollable rage resonated so strongly with our dark history of family violence that I slept that night at the train station in the freezing cold.

Back in Ethan's kitchen, my host continues, "But with George it was, here's how this works. Here, check this out. Let me show you what this does. And it was such a moving thing for me." Ethan has just finished brewing coffee and slides a cup in my direction. I ask for some sugar. He motions with his eyes to a small bowl nearby. I feel self-conscious as one . . . two . . . three . . . spoonfuls make their way into my cup, like he might be silently judging my sugar vice; silently keeping tabs on how many I sink into the cup's steaming depths—an impression that reflected my childhood years of living under the weight of my father's judgmental gaze. But when I look up, I see that Ethan is watching Georgina through the kitchen window as she mows the shaggy back lawn. "I get embarrassed," he says, quietly, shifting his gaze back to me. "It's really something I should do."

"That's not what I was thinking," I reply.

There's a brief silence, during which neither of us says anything. And then he returns his gaze to Georgina: "It's just one of those things. That kind of resentment does build because she does feel that way," the corner of his mouth turns up into a sardonic smirk, "even though she will deny it. But she thinks it: that I don't do what I'm supposed to do."

These days, Ethan sells toy collectables on eBay. His basement comprises three adjoining rooms: one has been converted into an office while the other two house his meticulously stored inventory. He admits that sometimes he feels like a "junk dealer," something like Fred Sanford from the '70s sitcom *Sanford and Son*, especially when he considers his once lucrative career in the toy industry. He spends the next ten minutes explaining that since "losing the house" and starting to work from home a few years ago he has still managed to keep a steady stream of income flowing into the house through his eBay business. The problem isn't that they're not making enough money, he tells me, but that they don't manage their money well: "That's the core of our problem."

PATRIARCHY AND MODES OF ATTUNEMENT

Parents are motivated and drawn to act as caregivers according to how they find themselves morally oriented in the world. Such orientations are acquired and shaped through gender-specific experiences and immersion in particular historio-cultural contexts. That is to say, from the time we are born we inhabit a time and place with others in which we learn with and through them the requisite skills, knowledge, and practices to successfully get along in the world—a world, I might add, that privileges and is patterned by and for certain *kinds* of bodies, according to their needs and interests. This is what Heidegger refers to as "being-in-the-world": the way I am always already involved in the world, which is disclosed in our understanding of the world and familiarity with the things in it.[1] Or, as Merleau-Ponty phrases it, "I am a psychological and historical structure and have received, with existence, a manner of existing, a style."[2] Thus, to be situated in the world is to find oneself already inhabiting a social milieu manifest in our habits, beliefs, aspirations, and expectations that reveal this cultural upbringing, only some of which we consciously cultivate.

We grow into a customary interpretation of ourselves, as Heidegger puts it, and grow up on that interpretation.[3] We project ourselves into possibilities that accord with how we understand ourselves against a sociohis-torical situation we did not choose.[4] The shared dimensions of our being-in-the-world are also deeply personal. Thus, it is my life, my responsibility, my concern, my care-for (X), and so on. In the case of fathers, there is no way to talk about the moral experiences of caregiving and their identi-ties as caregivers without exploring their histories of gendered experience and norms of masculinity that help to establish the parameters within which experience unfolds and articulates itself as meaningful. These fields within intersubjective life can be thought of as the constituting conditions against which we are acted upon and upon which we act throughout our lives as subjects.

Fathers' moral experiences around caregiving and projects of self-mak-ing are subtended and effected through their existential involvement in a wider patriarchal culture and prevailing gender norms and values that direct how we should understand ourselves and behave. As philosopher Linda Martín Alcoff argues, our complex intersectional identities make an epistemic difference, because they affect the kinds of experiences we have access to and the ways we are oriented to perceive and interpret them.[5] Thus, what we encounter in the world stands in relevance to what is disclosed in our understanding of the world, a relevance that is uncov-ered and made explicit by interpretation.[6] Thus, for Alcoff, identities are like horizons, because they provide background framing assumptions we bring with us to perception, understanding, and efforts to make sense of the world.[7] They often derive their reality from the fact that they are marked on the body, as she puts it, guiding the way we perceive and judge others and are perceived and judged by them.[8]

While simultaneous locations within social categories (education, race, gender, class, ability, sexual orientation, religion, etc.) differentially pat-tern subjective experience and access to power and privilege, my focus in the rest of this chapter is on how ideals of manhood and inclinations in thought and behavior engendered through a patriarchal value system—indeed, the very conditions for its maintenance and reproduction—are lived by fathers as "an obsessive presence, as possibility, enigma and myth," to borrow an evocative phrase from Merleau-Ponty.[9] I hope to show how expressions of fatherhood and masculinity often cohere around or fall out of sync with gender role expectations.

In Heideggerian terms, our possibilities of being attuned to things and the ways we interpret them always unfold against a background of shared everyday concerns and cultural practices. The various ways we are attuned to the world and others affect how we comport ourselves and the options we perceive for acting. As a basic structure of being embedded in the world, the concept of attunement is useful for considering a phenomenology of gendered experience and how fathers' worlds of care are shaped by an attunement to prevailing cultural notions of masculinity that often emphasize the subordination of empathy, the risk of vulnerability, and the value of control and recognition. The following stories help us understand how the personal disruption brought on by parenting a child with disabilities brings about wider disjunctions and ruptures, not least of which is the head-on exposure of the power of normative social and cultural patterns.

A DISCORDANT MELODY

My mother always said that if my father allowed her to manage the finances, then his businesses wouldn't have been liquidated. I remember waiting with my older sister after school under our regular pickup spot (a cherry plum tree). It was 1989 and I was eight years old. She was almost twelve, the age when most kids start to care a little more about their peers' perceptions. Eventually, my father arrived in a rusty old station wagon. I didn't pay much attention, but my sister asked where "our" car was, a blue 1988 Ford Fairlane. He defensively brushed her off, irritated. Little did we know that his business and assets had been liquidated, and the family car repossessed.

At that time, we lived a short drive away from my paternal grandparents. I remember spending a lot of time there. They were heavy smokers and their house smelled of stale cigarette smoke and other unidentifiable bits and pieces—a smell committed to my memory. My grandfather was a short and quiet man with a big cleft at the end of his nose. In most of my memories, he is sitting at the kitchen table in a haze of pale blue smoke underneath a large oil portrait of a lion with a steady gaze, staring out at the world from behind a painted veneer. He had come over from Scotland at fifteen and retained strong traces of brogue. He worked as a nurse educator most of his life and I'm told he was a charismatic and charming teacher, popular among the female nursing staff. But his popularity didn't extend beyond the hospital walls.

According to my mother, after he proposed, my grandmother's father, John, pinned my grandfather against the wall by the throat and forbade him to marry his daughter, threatening to sever ties with them if they went through with it. Idle were these threats beside the uniting force of love. They still got married. True to his word, my great-grandfather didn't speak to them again until after their three boys were born. Great-grandfather John died of an aneurism when my father was five. My father idolized him. He loved to tell and retell one tale in particular. It was a tale of retributive justice. One morning, John pulled up at a gas pump to refuel, when he saw a man at an adjacent pump kicking the shit out of his dog. When he was done, he threw the dog into the back of his truck like it was a threadbare tire. Before the sadist could settle in behind the steering wheel, John yanked him from the vehicle and delivered a series of solid kicks into his backside, driving him onto the pavement on all fours.

Whatever unity my grandparents possessed early on evaporated by the time stomach cancer ravaged my grandfather. After forty-odd years of catering to his needs, which culminated in a series of hospital admissions, my grandmother decided that rather than have him return home to her care some other community living situation would be more appropriate. After all the years of subservience, it was as if she were finally claiming the right to speak for herself. She called a family meeting at the hospital, where my father and his brothers agreed to support her decision. My father remembers his dad sitting in a wheelchair by himself in the hospital corridor, hands over his face, sobbing "like a child." He said seeing his dad like that was challenging. After all, this was a man who never cried. My grandfather was adamant that he didn't want to leave the house he had lived in for more than half his life. In the end, he didn't have to. He died a few weeks later in the hospital.

Growing up, my father often recounted living under his father's exclusive control and forbidding and mocking demeanor. My father entered a trade when he was sixteen and worked at steel mills and in metal construction for most of his life. When he was a young man, he would get into heated arguments with his father over who worked the hardest. For my grandfather, intellectual labor was the province of hard work. For my father, manual labor was the definition of man's work. In a cyclical turn of events, it turns out that my grandfather felt judged by his father who had worked manually all his life. History repeats itself, sometimes eerily so. In turn, my father would demean my career choice whenever he could.

"What are you up to?"

"Just working."

"Working? I wouldn't call that work!"

Even with these additional fragmentary sketches of my grandfather, it was hard for me to imagine him as anything outside of the solitary figure sitting at the table in smoke and stony silence.

My grandmother, on the other hand, was animated, warm, and funny. We had a meaningful connection based on our mutual love of "red dicks" (mini Frankfurters) and George Burns movies. But our time together was cut short. Not long after our Ford Fairlane mysteriously disappeared, my father did too. By that point, my four siblings and I had already been shipped off to live with my maternal grandmother. My father had a falling out with his parents over borrowed money he couldn't return; meanwhile, debts owed to townspeople had made him a local pariah. He resurfaced six months later once he had secured a job across the country, in the sub-urbs south of Fremantle in Western Australia. Soon, I was studying at a new school in Rockingham. I wasn't afforded the chance to say goodbye to my grandparents and I never saw them again.

My father always had an explosive temper, but there were stretches of time where things were ostensibly peaceful and there was no drama at home. But even then, I was constantly on guard. Physical and emotional violence were meted out for the slightest transgression. He didn't han-dle dissension well. There's one night that has stayed with me, though his treatment of me in this case was more subtle and less violent than I was used to. I was around nine at the time. A man of impetuous temper, on this occasion it was inflamed because I didn't thank him for a slice of pizza. He cornered me in the bathroom after my shower. I was hunched over naked and covering myself the best I could, and he was yelling that I was no longer his son. In a provocative move I threatened to leave the house. He cautioned that I would be leaving as naked as the day I arrived in this world since he had provided everything I owned. So, in the suit nature endowed me with, I made a break for it and hid outside behind a neighbor's car for ten minutes to see if he cared that I was gone. But it was my mother who appeared backlit in the open doorway, and my heart felt heavy.

AN ETHIC OF DOMINATION

Patriarchal culture wields immense influence over the ways men and women negotiate their gender identities, which are lived and enacted within and across fields of social difference and power. Like me, domestic violence robbed Ethan of a nurturing, teaching, respectful, and protective space to grow up in. Despite our social differences in class and environment—Ethan was from a middle-class background and from the American Midwest and I was from a working-class background in Australia—both our fathers embodied what feminist author bell hooks calls "dominator models of masculinity."[10] These dominator models, hooks states, collude with patriarchy as a sociopolitical system by valuing male power and a relation of domination, which upholds rigid and limiting understandings of power and maleness.[11] Through patriarchal gender relations and gendered performances, the ruling social structure plays out within our most intimate spaces. In phenomenological terms, these histories and lived experiences inform part of the background that structures the possibilities of gendered bodily experience and identity.

Ethan often lapsed into morose periods of introspection, descending into obstinate silence as he grappled with his complex and tormented inner life. He confessed to having both struck and abandoned his children. "I've been *both* fathers to him [Jack]," he admitted, which amounted to two of the worst incarnations of disorderly fathering, in his view. Careful attention to Ethan's vocabulary reveals connections to an earlier past where he was subjected to both failings by different men: abandoned by his biological father before he was six and abused by his stepfather. After a brief interregnum last year, during which he and Georgina lived apart for a short period, Ethan realized that he "crushed Jack" and was "being selfish." "I hated not being around," he recalled. "It was such an alien life for me. It was like losing myself. The stress was so enormous, but I couldn't live without it. It's been a totally different approach for me since I came back."

I am standing upstairs, in Ethan's bedroom. He reaches for a stack of drawings piled on top of a heavy, wooden desk and hands them to me. I sift through the illustrations, renderings of iconic superheroes and some new incarnations. Each illustration is pencilled with expert precision and detail. To the uninitiated, like myself, they are indistinguishable from the comics I collected as a boy. With pensive contemplation he tells the stories and events behind the illustrations, weaving them together, creating a temporal flow that highlights the evolution of his artistry and life; detailing his failure as a promising artist, his rise as the chief toy designer at a respected toy and collectables manufacturing and distributing company, and his ultimate shift to selling toy collectables on eBay from home and caring for Jack. He remarks that Georgina would prefer him to make the move back to full-time employment, an expectation that sits uneasily with what he feels are Jack's best interests: "The whole idea of working has affected my experience as a person and fills me with self-doubt and makes me question my value. Then, on the other hand, I feel like the path I took over the last eight years was good for Jack. So the expectations, I try and measure them, you know, are they mine or are they societal? Or are they my partner's? And then I put it into perspective. My thirtieth high school reunion is this year, OK? And one of the first thoughts I have is: I want to go but there's a part of me that is embarrassed to go because what do I say when someone says, what do you do? Which is a question people ask all the time. What do you do? I don't really know what I do. And the question has a complicated answer. And I don't know if people really want to hear it."

He laughs. "You know what I mean?"

"Have you rehearsed what the answer would look like?" I ask him.

"No. Maybe I should," he replies. "I guess you could say, I own my own business. But then there's the follow up question to that: what's your business? Well, I can't just say I sell junk on eBay, even though that's kind of what I do, because it's more complicated than that. And more interesting than that. If you have a job that's defined there's usually only one way to paint it, which is: I'm the chief operations officer of Think Way. Oh, how is that going for you? Good! The pay is good, and I have two weeks that they send me here and here, and I'm up for promotion in two months, and then you move on. I don't want to get involved in this complicated discussion about why the last eight years of my life I veered off from a career that was really good. Unless you want to. Because some people might be interested in the story. But some people might just want to hear that everything is fine."

Ethan and I are nearing the center of town, driving quickly to make Ethan's routine appointment with a chiropractor for his chronic back pain—the reason he can't do the "male defined" chores around the house, like mow the back lawn. He seems more at ease this morning. Maybe the chiropractor's ability to close the pain gates, even momentarily, brings him some peace of mind. He tells me that he attributes his failures in father-hood to the lack of positive fatherly influences in his life. "How do I be a better person, husband, father? I guess what I'm trying to do at forty-seven years old is find all the things my dad never gave me. Really, that's the truth. Before it's too late not to give those things to my kids."

This creates a segue into a description of a documentary on fatherhood that he watched recently, on the effects of fathers' absence on boys.

"This guy John Eldredge appears in this part of the documentary and I found him fascinating and so I started reading some of his stuff. He is of the mindset that the maleness of men is slowly being stripped away. It's an amazing book about how men have lost something, particularly our generation; I guess we're still in the same generation. Anyway, because of our upbringings and our dads were dumb, we didn't get some of these things that should have been put into us and what will happen, or the fear of what will happen, is we'll retract and the tendency will be to withdraw and not deal with things."

Ethan is talking about Christian masculinist writer John Eldredge, the author of *New York Times* best-selling book *Wild at Heart: Discovering the Secret of a Man's Soul.*[12] Eldredge's gender politics are in line with Christian masculinist values that manifest themselves in domina-tion, spurring men to reclaim the natural power of men over others. He emphasizes the importance of discovering the masculine soul. "Every man wants to play the hero," he writes, "Every man needs to know that he is powerful."[13] In referencing the documentary, Ethan aligns us both with Eldredge's notion of the undeveloped man: boys who, deprived of the love

and affirmation of fathers, consequently become spiritually and psycho-
logically broken, their potential to come alive as men left unrealized.[14]

Ethan's musings shed some light on how subjectivity and our moral
orientations are partially shaped by cultural productions and a tacit sense
of relatedness to others, which underpin the way we are affected by others, the choices we see for acting, and the expectations we hold about what
constitutes normal behavior. For Eldredge, gender identity is bestowed
by the father. "A boy learns if he is a man, if he has what it takes, from his
dad. A girl learns if she is worth pursuing, if she is lovely, from her dad.
That's just the way God set this whole thing up," he tells us.[15] The fundamental assumption underlying his paternalistic worldview is that men
and women have gender-specific capacities and styles of relating to others
that exist cross-culturally and are grounded in biological difference. As
Alcoff points out, the visibility of race and gender is often key to ideological claims that they are natural.[16]

Overall, for Eldredge, men derive meaning from their leadership and
productivity roles, while women derive their worth from relationships.
Thus, the biggest fear men harbor is failure in work and career, while
women fear abandonment.[17] In his view, journeying toward authentic
masculinity requires men to affirm their wild and aggressive masculinity
and take charge by fulfilling their benevolent responsibilities of leading,
protecting, and providing for their families. Despite the glaring hetero-
normative bias built into his worldview, a move toward masculine integrity and achieving a more emotionally fulfilling masculinity may seem
praiseworthy. In reality, however, Eldredge's vision of gender hierarchy
and the aggressive conflict that lies at the heart of his archetypal masculinity keep intact the social grounds of male identity rooted in an ethic of
superiority and domination. In contrast to a call for a more emotionally
fulfilling, honorable, and responsible masculinity, he enables the threat of
emasculation and an ethic of violence to remain guiding principles for the
ways in which men should construct their masculine selves.

How would Eldredge make sense of men who are inevitably dependent on others to have their needs met—through illness, disability, or old
age, for instance? Do they fall short of achieving manhood status because
of their inability to live up to his archetype of masculinity, inevitably relegated to a condition of enfeebled passivity? The claim that activity and

passivity are mutually exclusive reveals a paucity of imagination. There is no place in Eldredge's view for the kind of relational or moral equality that underpins social and political equality. Also, it neglects to see vulnerability as a core condition of humanhood, which can draw us closer to others and reveal our responsibility for each other.

Ethan's experiences as a father and man are beset by tensions and contradictions. He appears to be caught between the competing expectations enfolding postwar ideals of masculinity and fatherhood: between serving as the breadwinner for his family, on the one hand, and the expectation that fathers participate in the psychosocial development of their children, on the other.[18] At times, Ethan feels like he is fulfilling the cultural expectation to provide for his family through his eBay business; at other times, however, he feels this achievement is negated by his failure to climb a career ladder. Ethan's perceived failures to protect his children through his own failures and past punitive actions are also at odds with the cultural notion of the patriarch as a guiding and protective familial force—arguably, this has been exacerbated by a sense of vulnerability evoked by Jack's disability. And yet, as author Teresa McDowell writes, "Protecting and providing are contextually situated and depend on access to resources, *degree and type of family need*, political climate, and so on."[19]

Ethan's family situation and lived experience powerfully underscore McDowell's point. Ethan is drawn to Eldredge's account of authentic masculinity, which appears to enhance and give retrospective form to his experiences. Yet, the ethical demands of his family and its composition (and other debilitating physical ailments) continue to undermine this vision's validity. In short, his ideals of manhood and fatherhood implicitly clash and even devalue the care labor he is engaged in. The ever-increasing tension between fulfilling these ideals (i.e., healing the wounds of emasculation through the restoration of domestic patriarchy) and meeting the demands of his concrete situation, which include being responsive and attentive to Jack's needs, has induced an internal schism.

The felt weight of these moral gender expectations press in on Ethan's everyday experiences of fatherhood and caregiving, squeezing out their potentiality for an analytic reworking of his thoughts and emotions, or alternatives for thinking himself out of difficulty—rendering problematic his relationships with his wife and children in the process. His experience speaks to a time of moral breakdown: an experience where taken-for-granted values (to provide, to garner recognition, to lead his family) stand in tension with his specific situation and concern for Jack's care needs. Anthropologist Jarrett Zigon refers to these moments as ethical dilemmas: when our everyday moral mode of being-in-the-world breaks down and we are forced to step away and figure out the situation.[20] Zigon makes the distinction between morality as the unreflective mode of being-in-the-world and ethics as the conscious ethical tactics we perform in the moment of the breakdown to find resolution.[21] Thus, the primary goal of ethics, he suggests, "is to move back into the world; to once again dwell in the unreflective comfort of the familiar."[22] Herein lies Ethan's struggle as he engages in ethical questions, like what kinds of actions and ends are worth pursuing.

According to Ethan's ethical perspective, by virtue of being men, fathers contribute something irreplaceable to boys. Ethan confessed to "feeling castrated" because of his choice to work from home and play a larger part in caring for Jack: "I can't really fight that [feeling castrated] because I ended my career to care for Jack. To resurrect my career means to leave him. To take an alternate career means to diminish his care to whatever degree. I need to figure a lot of stuff out. Instead, I spend most of my time in avoidance." Interestingly, his renewed commitment to his family and responsive, attentive, and caring qualities do not figure into his self-perception as a man or father.

These gender norms were noticeable in the ways other fathers evaluated their situations too, and in their experiences of moral disequilibrium, like Doug, for instance, a father in his late forties who shared custody of his two autistic boys, Noah and Nick.

The first time I met Doug was at a support group for fathers in Chandler, an eastern suburb of Phoenix. Doug shuffled into the small conference room where Earl and I were sitting at a rectangular table that could have easily accommodated ten. He exuded a nervous and unpredictable energy that belied his solid frame, a look of someone who had pushed himself too far and was on the verge of collapse. In a weak economic climate with few job openings, Doug seemed to be staying afloat via odd jobs through his church and the monetary support he received from family. He admitted to feeling "emotionally drained." The combination of living alone, working and hustling, caring for the boys, stress eating, and the pressure of being behind in child support payments had led to a recent spate of cardiac palpitations, according to Doug. He feared these palpitations were an ominous sign of something worse to come, something like God sounding the final eviction notice. But they turned out to be nothing.

Doug revealed that, when his children were first diagnosed, he thought, "I gotta live to be a hundred and twenty years old so I can outlive my kids. I gotta take care of my kids. That was the mindset from day one." Later, he adds, "It pains me in some respect that as a man I can't provide [private therapy] that for my kids and I hate being dependent on the government. But we are. That's where we are. I don't know how many people I have thanked over the years for paying their taxes." Months later, a scan of the titles on the spines of the books on his bookshelf affirm this felt moral expectation: *Lead the Field, Learn to Earn, The Courage to Be Rich, Acres of Diamonds.*

Doug's and Ethan's experiences and reflections speak to the ways their constructions of fatherhood and manhood bear on their experiences of caregiving, which are sometimes disclosed in relation to ideals of breadwinning and success in the marketplace. Their inability to access the power, privilege, and status conferred through participation in the formal economy has left them feeling discredited as both men and fathers. As author Michael Schwalbe notes, "The benefits and rewards of manhood status compel all males to claim it, even against conscience."[23]

During the support meeting, mid-conversation, Doug reveals that he's recently joined a men's group. Before he can drift too far from his remark, I ask:

"What men's group?"

"It's a twelve week—it's kind of hardcore. Most Bible studies are like eighty percent Bible and twenty percent, you know, relationship touchy-feely stuff. This is biblically based, like twenty percent focus on the Bible and the other eighty percent is like hardcore."

"Like Fight Club?" I ask, but inside I am eager to excavate the deeper layers of what he is saying.

Earl and Doug laugh together.

"Yeah, it's really intense. You have to sign a thing saying you won't talk about anything you do—"

"What kind of things do you do?" I ask.

Earl interjects, laughing, "Not talk about it."

Doug laughs a bit and continues, "We just get into the meat of things, you know."

"Where is this?" Earl asks.

"Men of Valor."

Earl nods, "Oh, OK. Yeah."

"You've heard of it?" Doug asks.

"Yes. Yep," Earl nods, encouragingly.

"Is it a similar kind of group to the one you attend?" I ask Earl.

"Rebel? No. Well, it's a lot of the same concepts but it's—Men of Valor is more structured. Rebel is more free flowing. It's men getting up to share their testimony, their story, getting in your face with stuff they've dealt with in life. We sit around and get in each other's faces in regard to what was talked [about]."

Doug says, "And typically you have about enough people in it that every week someone really takes time to spill their guts and really open up and just—I mean, I've seen some really really tough men just bawling, you know, through these meetings. The first time I went through, man, I was crying a lot."

"What do you hope to get out of the experience?" I ask.

"Honestly, I'm not sure why I even went." Doug emits a constrained laugh, like he's afraid he might burst a pair of sutures. "I was just in need of communication and relationship because I had been out of work for months and, um, just really starting to lose—just turning into jelly and, you know, really needed some guys to rally around and in turn rally around them, to be a part of that and in it."

The hypermasculine language employed by Earl and Doug is revealing. It's illustrative of the ways men shift in and out of their masculine identities, just like their caregiving ones, according to the situations they inhabit with others. But we can also see that the material and symbolic rewards conferred though participation and success in the workplace are not the only things at stake here. Doug's own self-perceived credibility as a man and a sense of how he measures up to other men also seem to figure prominently in the ways he defines himself as man. Doug's dependency on state support and benefits and inability to prove himself in the workplace have engendered feelings of failure and shame. Arguably, his participation and acceptance in a group of "tough" guys enable him to continue feeling like a man, satisfying his self-perceptions and his relational value vis-à-vis other men. Through his participation in Men of Valor, Doug is able to maintain membership in the dominant gender group.

Earl's description of group participation at Rebel and "getting in each other's faces" defines a particular style of interaction, one charged with aggression. Perhaps these expressions of hypermasculinity serve to ward off any affronts to their sense of manhood that emotionally intimate conversations around vulnerability, pain, and care—woven into the fabric of group discussion—give rise to. These moments disclose the ways men are embedded in a set of shared patriarchal cultural practices, patterns of saying and doing embodied in their socially derived dispositions to act in certain ways in particular situations, guiding what actions matter to them and how they relate to themselves and others.

A DISCORDANT MELODY (CONT'D)

I learned early on that my father's identity as a man and father was anchored in his instrumentality as the breadwinner of the family. But my father's excessive investment in the symbolic capital that breadwinning provided came before other expressions of care (physical, emotional, or intellectual). Of course, breadwinning does not negate one's ability to express care. Indeed, the role of economic provider itself can be thought of as a form of care, supportive of another's care labor. But even so, this rarely involves hands-on care activities, because according to the ideology of the male breadwinner family, caregiving is subordinate to providing care in economic terms. My father would have felt more guilt about losing economic opportunities than the little time he spent with us. In his case, the male breadwinner/female caregiver logic lent itself too easily to the emotional distance that accommodated his absence and abuse.

Early on I learned that dissension in the ranks would not be tolerated and that my father's position of dominance within the household would be maintained through physical and emotional violence. When business liquidation and debt threatened his masculine identity, particularly his economic authority and sense of hard work, he was prepared to restore his masculine self-worth and position as head of the household at whatever cost necessary, whether that meant disappearing for lengthy periods of time or estranging his children from loved ones who threatened him with emasculation through economic dependency. By the time I was six I understood that my father's displays of dominance were undermining our relationship and negatively affecting how I felt toward him. In fact, these early experiences would affectively load many of my future relationships and survive in my body's permanent readiness for conflict.

For a short while before my parents' divorce, we lived as a family—my father, my mother, my two sisters, my two brothers, and I. A man of habit, my father would leave early for work each morning and return in the evening, tired, disgruntled, and entitled. He demanded solitude, peace, and quiet, spending the next hour or so hunched over a beer and talking quietly with my mother in the kitchen or playing Nintendo until she called him for dinner. During our family dinners we would sit in a clenched atmosphere, for whoever committed a transgression that day would surely fall into his crosshairs as the object of his bitter tirades and table thumping. He worked hard as the sole breadwinner to keep us financially afloat and I imagine this wore down his patience. But what could have been for him an interlude of respite from the pressure and grind of the everyday was instead spent fulfilling his duties as the disciplinarian.

His energies and time spent working accompanied a rise in living standards and the flourishing pleasures of materialism. He once remarked with resentment that we never went on holidays as a family when I was growing up because he poured his earnings into the house and accommodating my mother's materialist demands. Like many men throughout the twentieth century in capitalist societies, my father's status and position of privilege within the home were tied to his participation within wider systems of domination. "Be a man," Schwalbe says men are told, "be strong, ambitious, potent, competitive, achieve wealth, status, and power; get ahead of others, and do not let yourself be dominated."[24] Yet, as he rightly points out, most men fail at claiming manhood status based on success and power in the workplace, the economic and political realities of a capitalist society being what they are. I have no doubt my father compensated for this sense of powerlessness within the workplace by tightening his grip upon the authoritarian reins of control at home.

There were other political and economic changes afoot that perhaps threatened his sense of control and unspoken privilege—for example, increases in women's employment, expansion of publicly supported child-care, and increasing divorce rates all fostered the emergence of new family compositions. These wider social shifts began to undermine the cultural ideal of the modern nuclear family represented by the two-parent, gen-der differentiated household—itself a product of particular historical and social time. And by the time of my childhood in the 1980s, the economic and social terrain had been shifting for some time. Australia witnessed increased changes in patterns of work that signalled a new economic order: from an industrial to a postindustrial era.[25] The economic future would no longer be based on the labor-intensive factory production that my father perceived as a "real man's work," but on high-technology infor-mation industries.

Looking back on it now, our family structure was organized around three principles: breadwinning, heterosexuality, and hierarchical author-ity—and to varying degrees I recognized these same expressions of patri-archy within the homes of my friends growing up. In action, these prin-ciples functioned to uphold my father's position of superiority, privilege, and authority within and outside the home (to varying degrees), asserting his claims to respect among us and warding off displacements that threat-ened to disturb his credibility as a man. He didn't hesitate to feminize or express disdain toward people or things that threatened to undermine his sense of manliness and level of comfort: from white-collar "pencil pushers" who signified his subjugation to his father and acted as a screen against which he defined his brand of masculinity, on the one hand, to his open and frowning disdain for my love of movies and acting over football and fishing, on the other. As psychologist Aaronette White puts it, "Each subgroup of men defines manhood in ways that conform to the economic and social possibilities of that group."[26] These hierarchies that preserve patriarchy, she points out, create alienation and isolation among men so that most men will end up colluding with the system to experience any sense of power and control.[27]

My father drew on the symbolic resources available to him in substan-tiating his masculinity. With little formal education, he put great stock in his strength and virility. His definition of manliness was incarnated by all his favorite action heroes of the time (Stallone, Seagal, Schwarzenegger,

Van Damme—the glory years of action cinema!) But his ideals were also implicitly articulated in the stories he told me growing up, stories that were grounded in retributive violence or other heroic feats that bolstered his virtues of manliness. One story was typical: once, a freak tidal wave threatened to absorb me and my father, and we dangled above the thunderous sea, huge waves lashing the rocks below. With one hand clamped around a sharp rock outcropping and the other around my infant body, he eventually managed to pull us both to safety, single-handedly. According to my parents, I would have met certain death if left in the literal hands of certain *kinds* of men who had not cultivated his mettle and physical strength through hard manual labor.

My father's enactments of manhood were an exercise in contradiction and ambiguity. Despite his perceived independence and self-sufficiency, he relied, or rather took for granted, the care work of my maternal grandmother and her unquestionable willingness to let us live with her. Care ethicist Joan Tronto has termed this type of behavior "privileged irresponsibility."[28] It is one of many patriarchal privileges, and in this particular instance it speaks to my father's structural privilege as a man to pursue his economic goals by disappearing for protracted lengths of time while excusing himself from the responsibilities of care labor at home. During these times he was the beneficiary of my maternal grandmother's support and good will. He never thanked her for the times she took us in over the years and I doubt he ever felt like he should. This is how privileged irresponsibility works; it is invisible and like other hegemonic mechanisms relies on its invisibility to sustain and naturalize power relations.

There were other behaviors that contrasted uneasily with the archetypal emotional stoicism and self-control my father aspired to. Once, when I was fifteen, my brother and I stood outside his apartment in the dark, waiting for our mother. They had only been separated for a few months at the time. It was clear by their gestures that they were involved in a serious conversation. He visibly embodied some powerful emotion, and my mother started edging back toward the door. Winded by emotional pain, my father, a man of formidable proportions, dropped to his knees, felled by the same human vulnerability that unites us all. My brother and I exchanged a silent look of shared surprise and discomfort. And then we mocked him for "crying like a bitch."

TOKENS OF PRIVILEGE

Many of the families I spent time with illustrated the variability in caring arrangements that are negotiated according to practical demands and constraints, economic resources, marital and family status, relationships, access to support and services, and which are patterned according to attitudes and obligations along the lines of race/ethnicity, class, religion, disability, and gender. Despite the degree of flexibility in family caring arrangements, patterned as they are by differences in intersectional identities, the shared cultural practices of caring and earning that guide how men and women understand their moral identities as fathers and mothers figured prominently in the lives of the caregivers I spent time with—highlighting what these practices take for granted, namely, the nature of male-female relations. Traditionally caring has been viewed as natural to women, "intrinsic to their femininity," as anthropologists Tamara Kohn and Rosemary McKechnie write, and has, "therefore . . . been defined by conceptual dichotomies which have ordered a division of labour, naturalized moral responsibilities, maintained the low status of caring."[29]

The conflation of motherhood and female normalcy wrought by patriarchy works to naturalize the unpaid care work women engage in. Ethan commented, "The guy mindset is a bit fragile as far as being able to process complex emotions. This is what I think: women are just better equipped to handle very difficult circumstances in the family and men tend to run from it." Inherent in his remark is an essentializing assumption about the maternal capacities and inclinations of women. According to this gendered worldview, women are naturally endowed with the feminine (emotional) qualities necessary to care for a disabled child. Failing to live up to one's natural feminine vocation, then, can often be judged by society as symptomatic of moral incompetence. Essentialist assumptions of this variety serve a patriarchal agenda by wedding women to domesticity and care labor.

In his research on men and care work in Ireland, Hanlon found that such essentializing rhetoric provides men with a rationale to avoid care work.[30] Thus, those who choose to involve themselves in this kind of work do so because they feel emotionally equipped to cope.[31] However, as he points out, "narratives of choice" are myopic, because they locate "the source of action upon free acting individuals unencumbered by structural constraints."[32] "Care choices are facilitated by a gender regime," he writes, "that legitimates what is desirable cultural and emotional capital of men and women."[33] The fathers in my study are engaged in a higher amount of hands-on caregiving than is typical of fathers across North America. Despite their nonconformance to traditional gender practices and normative expectations, however, the privilege conferred upon them for being men is discernible in many areas, in processes of exchange and accommodation.

In the previous chapter, Doug said, "I hear it's dads who leave because they can't deal with their kids." Indeed, many of the fathers I spent time with quoted the same statistic, that there is an 80 percent divorce rate in marriages where the parents are raising a disabled child. There is no question that women have traditionally borne the responsibility of caregiving—which Kittay attributes to "a legacy of tradition, of sexism, and of a sexual taboo against men being involved in the intimate care of women's bodies"[34]—and continue to bear the major responsibility for providing care for disabled children in North America. Regardless of whether the divorce rate is 50 or 80 percent, traditional family values and the commonly held belief in the pervasiveness of high divorce rates in families raising disabled children influence the ways the fathers in this book view themselves and are viewed by others: as anomalies. As exceptions to the rule, then, they are often commended by their spouses and others for their caregiving efforts and commitments to their families. These commendations are unidirectional, unmasking social expectations concerning female morality and the moral obligation socially assigned to women to assume caregiving responsibilities. What does this say about the perceived state of manhood, when one's commitment to family and emotional intimacy with one's child are heralded as exceptions rather than the rule?

Throughout my interactions with the families involved in the study, I witnessed both spouses construct masculinist narratives that explained a father's committed presence and ability to deal with the tribulations of caring for a disabled child, described to me by one couple as resembling the kind of fortitude that is cultivated in ranching in Alaska's Aleutian Islands. Often these narratives did the work of upholding fathers' masculine identities as caregivers and cohered around prevailing cultural images of masculinity that dominate the US cultural landscape, which involve a denial of vulnerability and emphasize autonomy, strength, and resilience. In these and many other ways, fathers receive recognition and sometimes praise for doing what women are socially expected to do to fulfill their vocations of proper motherhood.

Another systematic advantage conferred to men relates to the ways they are lauded when they bring their personal stories into public spheres. These stories often contribute to broader conversations around disability and offer counternarratives of hope in the face of unexpected disruption. They inevitably foreground the commitments and sacrifices involved in caring for a disabled child. This cultural activity, however, unmasks the unequal distribution of power and privilege between men and women. For example, men who have established a public presence for themselves through participation in the paid labor force are afforded opportunities to share their stories and participate in speaking engagements that are not made available to their spouses who have, in many instances, shouldered a lot more domestic responsibility than they have over the years.

A DISCORDANT MELODY (CONT'D)

Over time, my father was pulled further adrift through the expression of rigid gendered meanings. In the end, his relentless pursuit of dominance contributed to the ruination of our family unit. It seemed to me that neither my father, nor his, understood the personal costs extracted by the demands of patriarchal masculinity and living up to its illusory ideals; a point well expressed by hooks when she writes, "Patriarchy demands of men that they become and remain emotional cripples."[35] True to the impermanence and flux of life, the domination and power conferred through traditional patriarchal relations are often seriously undermined by illness and/or aging: the patriarch falls, or in the case of my grandfather, sits sobbing in a hospital corridor alone, bereft of intimate connections.

During a regrettably brief period of reconciliation during my early thirties, I noticed a gentler side to my father. It was hard for me to tell whether time cultivated it or if it had always been there underneath his veneer of stoicism. Perhaps. But most likely its seeds were suffocated under the anaerobic conditions of patriarchal manhood. There is no doubt in my mind that my father's tumultuous relationship with his own father provided the earliest experiences from which he began to understand himself as a man. They also formed parts of the ground that established his gendered orientation in the world: his hopes and fears, prejudices and aversions. In fact, everything he aspired to was in contradistinction to his father, except the very thing that made them the most alike: their will to power.

As hooks reminds us, both women and men teach this dominator model of relating to children, and patriarchal ideology gripped my mother's consciousness too.[36] She turned a blind eye to his careless practices. In her patriarchal logic, my father was acting in the ways socially expected of him as the patriarch and breadwinner of the family: he provided us with a home, kept food on the table, and never "denied her" more children (they had five). This breadwinner-homemaker ideal is not only powerful in aligning manhood with the public realm but also increases a father's recognition and supremacy within the home because of the sacrifices he makes.

For over twenty-three years my mother submitted to her perceived biological destiny and tailored her feelings and desires to his. According to her, she had taken her rightful place in the natural social order and had fulfilled the feminine and natural vocation assigned to her as mother and wife. She devoted over two decades of her life in service to the practical and emotional needs of her husband and children. My mother renounced her sovereignty when she married my father at the age of seventeen. I don't think she had time to experience the "agonizing dilemma" that French writer and feminist philosopher Simone de Beauvoir suggests the "woman-to-be" must struggle with until much later; that is, the conflicts that arise between a woman's "originary claim to be subject, activity, and freedom, on the one hand and, on the other...the social pressure to assume herself as a passive object."[37] But in the end my mother yearned for more outside her marriage and the lot assigned to her in patriarchy. I got the sense that a great ambivalence grew from the chasm that time slowly opened between her "properly human condition and her feminine vocation."[38] Years after her divorce from my father, she would reflect despairingly on the stifling conditions of her marriage and would celebrate her freedom, activity, and desire.

Of course, family life is only one of many avenues through which we are exposed to dominant cultural beliefs and practices that govern how we should think and feel about our gender identities—others include the media, pornography, religion, and schooling. Gender policing is a persistent experience in the lives of men and starts as early as school, where male identities are surveilled and policed by peers who set the standards against which one's actions are measured and judged. Often, transgressing these gender boundaries or failing to supress expressions that do not conform to domineering forms of masculinity result in violence and ridicule. "Masculinizing violence," as anthropologist Guillermo Núñez Noriega puts it, creates fear and adherence to "the project of becoming a man."[39]

I remember being bullied in fourth grade for taking pride in my hair. My Elvis pompadour invited verbal homophobic taunts and random episodes of physical assault by older boys. Teachers advised my parents that the torments would most probably stop if they discouraged my stylistic rockabilly inclinations. At home, I was taught to fight back, and that retaliatory violence was a legitimate expression of my maleness. This advice proved useful, as my acceptance at every new school I attended growing up hinged upon my ability to prove myself to my fellow brethren through my capacity to do violence when provoked—and it never failed to get me in my father's good graces. Like other mediums of socialization, masculinizing violence operates under a cloak of invisibility and appeared quite natural to me early on.

EXISTENTIAL AND MORAL ORIENTATIONS

I was fifteen minutes late getting to the Mediterranean Grill in Mesa, Arizona, where I was meeting Gary for lunch—Route 101 was congested and a trip to the pharmacy to inquire about a weeping rash Takoda had developed across his face delayed my departure. Gary was sitting at a booth by the window in front of a cup of soda when I arrived. Except for a couple of other patrons, we had the place to ourselves. I enjoyed Gary's company and his unique blend of humor and insight. In a past life he was a teacher—he had an MA in history and had taken some classes back in his twenties at the university I attended back home in Melbourne.

"Melbourne reminds me a lot of Portland, Oregon," he tells me.

He reminisces about his time spent there, drinking beer and playing pool at a hotel I'm familiar with, just around the corner from the university. I ask if he gets the chance to travel these days and he replies gently, "With Mia it's too difficult." I didn't understand then, the way I do now, how difficult traveling with a severely disabled child becomes over time: the logistical nightmare of maneuvering bodies and wheelchairs, transporting a breadth of supplies (diapers, food, medicine, equipment), securing a vehicle with enough space to accommodate said wheelchair and supplies, and trying to secure accommodation with the appropriate bedding (with guard rails, etc.).

Gary moved to Arizona fourteen years ago with his wife to take up a teaching position at a charter school. He tells me he's acclimated to the hot desert weather but misses the restaurants back in Portland. After Mia's injury, though, he made the transition to being her primary caregiver. Cherry stayed on working full-time because she was earning more than Gary; a decision that, he admits, sometimes weighs heavily on her moral conscience. Gary didn't appear to be burdened in the same way as Cherry by the prescribed social meanings that index our social identities as fathers and mothers. He reveals in a cavalier manner that Cherry sometimes picks up on subtle deprecations from others when they learn he is Mia's primary caregiver: a disapproving look or gesture, to which he admits being oblivious.

Like other fathers in this study (including myself), the meanings of fatherhood for Gary, the values and motives stitched into his thoughts and actions, cohere around his experiences growing up. "I didn't want to be anything like my dad," he says. "I wanted to be as financially successful as my dad, but he's not a very demonstrative person. He doesn't hug a lot, you know. He doesn't even smile a lot or laugh a lot or anything like that. And I think he learned that from his dad, who grew up in the forties; he was an old Polish guy that came from the old country. You know, so he wasn't demonstrative. And I never understood how you could live your life like that."

The waiter brings over two chicken kabob pitas. Gary takes a mouthful and launches straight back in:

"He's not a bad dad, at all. It's just his attitude is to provide financially and everything else is mom's job. Like, he's complimented me once in my life and I remember it 'cause it was only once and I was stunned: I got a really good grade point average in my first year of college and I got my transcript and he was like, good job! I was like, who are you?" He breaks into a rolling chuckle. "And so, when I was growing up, I was like, I am not going to be like him. I don't want to be that kind of person with my kids. And I'm not that kind of person. We did a lot of good things growing up and he was never appreciative of it. It was like he didn't care. How do you live your life like that? I would play soccer, I wasn't very good at soccer, and maybe win, maybe lose, but if we won, like two to one, that was golden. He'd talk about the one I gave up and why I didn't do a better job. And I'm like, we won the game!" He laughs again defensively.

"True," I respond.

"I have consciously tried to be more accessible. I think you have to be empathetic. I don't mean to sound like an arrogant jerk, but I don't know why I am that way because, like I said, dad was not really there. He wasn't an emotional part of the equation. He's a good guy. He's not like, you know, touchy-feely. I don't know if it was my mum. She's very, you know, I would call her a good Christian—as opposed to an evil Christian," he says self-mockingly. "But she's a very nice person. She wants to help other people, that sort of thing. I don't know if it's that. I have no idea. But I've always been empathetic. I really have."

When I asked fathers in the study to reflect on some of the experiences they think may have contributed to their caring orientations, they often responded through recourse to their fathers. During these conversations background gender assumptions often came to the fore, a taken-for-granted sense of how men felt themselves belonging to the world. The conflation of male sexed bodies with attributions of masculinity often wedded men to the significance and influence of their fathers when reflecting on their lives as caregivers. I found that this sense of reality often constrained their thinking in particular ways, curtailing, for instance, their appreciation for the great variety of influences that may in fact have shaped their orientation to the world. Gary alludes to the possibility of his mother's influence, but it is the significance of his father around which his thoughts circle. Consequently, the men in my study often enact fathering in favor of or resistance to their own fathers and normative models of fatherhood. Paul offered an interesting exception.

His father had been a college football star ("fleet footed," according to a local newspaper). He earned a degree in physical education and was a fighter-bomber pilot and captain in the US Strategic Air Command during the Korean War. Later in life, he worked in the pharmaceutical industry (very early on as a pharmaceutical sales rep selling Mylanta) until his retirement in the 1990s. "He was a great man," Paul recalls, "emotionally available if we needed him to be." He succumbed to dementia in his final years and his increasing dependency and helplessness had been a difficult blow for someone who had always been so independent, Paul tells me, and a crushing blow for his wife who had always known him to be so. She cared for him until his death in 2010. By that time, they had been married sixty-two years.

"She's a very special person," Paul says about his mother, as we drive to the local farmer's market. "Her father died when she was six and her mother had to work. As a child she used to come home to an empty house. So my mother insisted on being home every day when I got home from school. Then, in eleventh grade, with tears in her eyes she asked me if it was OK if she went to work—to pay for my college. I said, Ma, I don't need you at home when I get home from school. I tell you that because for sixteen years I was home every day for when Pearl got off the bus. My mother influenced me greatly."

The accounts I have sketched of Gary and Paul make visible the extent to which our existential and moral orientations are influenced and shaped by our interactions with others and shared forms of life. Parents' worlds of disability are disclosed as mattering in particular ways, as bearing imports. And these imports motivate commitments, choices, and actions.

It took Earl some years before he noticed his restrictive ideas of manhood had permeated his emotional encounters with the world. He set himself adrift from his family by plunging himself into work and taking "care of the things that men do." By seeking refuge in masculine ideals of earning and providing for his family, Earl attempted to distance himself from the care labor Zachary depended on and the abiding imprint of grief.

As time would have it though, he eventually lost a sense of fulfillment that came with the habitual expectation of breadwinning, and the influence of the appointed gender order he was at grips with became a little clearer and more comprehensible. Earl realized that if he wanted to be the kind of father that Zachary *needed* him to be, rather than the kind of father he felt he *ought* to be, then he would have to shift his priorities and commit himself to being more present and involved with family life, foregoing the restrictive notions of manhood from which he had arrived at an understanding of himself and his relationship to others.

Earl's repudiation of old patterns may seem surprising, especially given his convictions that caring for his disabled father robbed him of a childhood. But the disjuncture between his everyday mode of being and Zachary's needs constituted an ethical dilemma that he had to work through and attempt to reconcile. This can be thought of as a time of moral breakdown that threw him out of sync with his habitual attunement to things and prompted him to reflect upon his moral comportment in a new light.

MORAL BREAKDOWN AND AWAKENINGS

Doug is what is often referred to as a "military brat." His father, Bill, served in the military (two tours in Vietnam) and so he experienced the kind of nomadic upbringing that befalls most military children, relocating homes every year or so. This nomadism walled him off from establishing long-lasting connections to others. He never settled in any one place long enough to make friends or to forge the kind of connections to space that create a sense of home. His only enduring point of reference was a lithograph hanging on the wall depicting a dilapidated barn in a vast expanse of nothingness, caught somewhere between sunrise and sunset.

Once, during a support meeting, he confessed to me and Earl that his biggest fear, before having children and discovering his own autism, was that his future progeny would be born autistic. Earl suggested that God was making him face his own autism, that He had chosen him specifically as the boys' father for the knowledge he possessed as an autistic person. Doug passively accepted this. But I wondered at the time if the pro-pounded emotional elusivity of autistic children invoked a fear of further alienation in Doug, a fear of feeling disconnected from his own children, those most firmly within his orbit.

Doug was barely inside the door and removing his coat one night when he heard his father's voice in the adjoining room. It was charged with frustration.

"You're not listening to me!"

From the doorway, Doug could see Bill sitting at the oval kitchen table with Noah. They were working on a jigsaw puzzle together. The problem was Noah wasn't quite as locked-in on the project as Bill; instead, his eyes were fixed to the television in the den.

"Noah?" Bill let out a gusty sigh and leaned back in his chair, arms crossed.

Doug has immense respect for his father (an eighty-year-old ex-Marine who could still do one-armed push-ups) and, unlike his other siblings, still depends on his parents for financial support. "I've probably wiped out whatever inheritance they [his siblings] had," Doug joked one warm August night as we stood in the parking lot of Mi Amigo's Mexican Grill in Mesa. Bill was rarely outwardly angry, according to Doug, but he was a man with obsessive idiosyncrasies: exhibiting an authoritarian style and prizing composure and efficacy above all else. To Doug, Bill's manner of fathering was at odds with Noah's best interests and needs.

"Noah?" Bill repeated.

Doug focused his quiet desperation on Bill. He was impelled to say something. But he didn't know what. Surely words would help clear the path of revelation cutting its way through his body. Finally, he said, "Dad, can I talk to you outside for a minute?"

Bill followed him outside.

"I know you don't mean any harm, OK. But you can't talk to him like that," Doug said.

Bill shifted his weight slightly, guarded but attentive.

Doug continued, "Everything I thought I knew about parenting went out the window when these boys were born. The ways that might have worked for you when we were growing up won't work for them. You can't talk to him like that."

. . . . .

I was thirty when my son was born. It was evident by the time he was four months old that he was disabled. There is perhaps nothing more gut-wrenching and disorienting, I learned, than watching your infant in the throes of neuronal chaos, seized by electrical impulses gone awry. Multiple times a day, his tiny body would stiffen and turn red; his altered state of consciousness holding me (and him) in interstitial suspension, between the known and unknown, between stability and chaos. Afterward, I would hold his limp body in my hands, havoc roiling inside, a contradictory muddle of self-pity and the profoundest fellow feeling imaginable. As Takoda grew older and his disabilities more profound, I grieved losing the opportunity to raise a son the way I had envisioned. I grieved the lost opportunity to raise a boy who would be emotionally perceptive, attentive, and responsive to the needs of others. My familiar everyday world was shattered by this utterly dependent body and the promises I thought parenthood had failed to deliver on.

When my son was two years old, my eldest brother posted a meme on his Facebook page that contained obvious ableist undertones. I hastily confronted his complicity in spreading ableist bigotry. Giving him the benefit of ignorance, I asked him to remove it from his Facebook page. He responded quickly with defensive aggression, as though his manhood were on the line. At first, he cut off all communication. Then days later, on a Saturday night, he responded with a text: *what are you going to fucking do about it? You can't do shit. And neither can your son!*

The statement hit its intended mark. It induced a readiness for conflict and violence that was familiar to me, sedimented through traumatic childhood experiences. With my blood thumping in my ears and my body tensing to the point where it was hard to breathe, my indignation grew, robbing me of the latitude to think. I was angry that my son had been unjustifiably attacked and devalued. And my manhood had been challenged through my brother's insinuation of cowardice. I was clenched in a trembling state of rage. Broiling with anger and hurt, endowed with confidence from a decade of Thai boxing, I planned to drive to his house and prove to him *what* I could do.

I don't know what it was that stopped me. At the time, my son was aimlessly rummaging among his toys, happily and repetitively stroking them with his fingers.[40] By then, my partner and I had a daughter too. She was lying on her back, intently watching her brother. I believe it had something to do with caring for them, something of the intimacy involved, which had expanded my outer world; my children had existentially increased my emotional range. Years of caregiving had pressed upon my identity as a man, giving rise to an existential tension between my newfound self-esteem and the way I still resonated in affect to the patriarchal demands of securing recognition and resisting control—a particular way of being morally attuned to things.

By the time I was fourteen I clearly recognized that I didn't want to be anything like my father, and my mother often assuaged these unarticulated anxieties by emphasizing our physical and dispositional differences. But even as she renounced my father's oppressive grip of domination and control over her, plunging herself into economic uncertainty, she continued desiring and dating men who expressed in belief and action the same patriarchal ethos he did. And the same contradictions shrouded my moral experiences. I was repulsed by my father's restrictive brand of masculinity and valorization of dominance and, yet, I had incorporated bits of the same signifying behavior into my own performance of manhood. I was defending what I thought was a credible masculine self: resisting control and asserting dominance.

Months passed and the anger sat quietly on the margins of my awareness. A dysphoria colored my experience of the world and kept me awake at night. I experienced an emotional bipolarity, wherein I oscillated between feeling compelled to retaliate and do what I ought to do as a man or honoring the feelings of dignity and strength I had discovered through caregiving and being with my son (and daughter). I was pulled between the demands of participation in a violent and controlling male culture—which inherently diminishes the power and worth of individuals who do not conform to oppressive patriarchal golden standards—or honoring alternate expressions of manhood that would nurture the kinds of values I wanted to inhabit as a father: accountability, strength, integrity, trustworthiness, and a high regard for love; expressions that would create the kind of emotionally safe and protective space I wanted my children to grow up in.

This incident with my brother forced me to sit in silent communion with my consciousness. I realized that I was different in degree from my father, but not in kind. The episode elicited a profound sense of indignation—steeped in paternalism?—that I was going to use to justify my violent ends. My vulnerability had been exploited and I was responding through masculine dominance. And what could be more masculine than the retributive violence I envisioned? I didn't want to live in my father's shadow or perpetuate the toxic behaviors and practices that nurtured its growth. Furthermore, I came to realize that by continuing to inhabit the world in this way, I was tied up in maintaining the same exploitative social hierarchies that undermine Takoda's value and are antithetical to expressions of care and the spirit of communal mutuality that would nurture his well-being (and that of others like him).

Several years later, while on my doctoral fieldwork in Norfolk County, Massachusetts, I was unknowingly infected with the spirochaete bacterium, *Borrelia burgdorferi* (Bb): the etiological agent of Lyme disease. These cork-screwed shaped bacteria enter the bloodstream and disseminate to multiple sites throughout the body. I experienced muscle and joint pain, muscle twitching, nocturnal seizures, cardiac abnormalities, depression, fatigue, and substantial neuropsychiatric disturbances. Lyme disease is a shape-shifting illness, and symptoms can vary. Early on, the confluence of symptoms confounded medical professionals. It took almost twelve months before the Centers for Disease Control and Prevention diagnosed me with Lyme disease. My illness, much like the arrival of a child who deviates from neuropsychological and physiological norms, punctured my familiar world and cast my life into uncertainty. This amounted to a loss of control over my life and caused immense despair and anxiety.

My ordinary patterns of everyday life deteriorated. The world around me no longer hummed with vibrancy or possibility. I couldn't climb a short flight of stairs without almost collapsing, forget about kickboxing. I no longer had the stamina to play with my children or take care of them the way I was used to doing. The roles and responsibilities that shored up my identity as a father and caregiver were lost to me. I became dependent on my spouse for care. Being a caregiver was an important part of the way I understood myself. I was living a life of equality and intimacy which, in my mind, differentiated me from the likes of my father. I was in a relationship based on equality and respect, which separated it from the strange and, at times, perverse union that characterized my parents' marriage. My illness advanced to the point where it held me hostage inside my bedroom. I'd fallen down a rabbit hole and the anxiety engendered by having entered this altered reality, the fear of never finding my way out again, was almost too much to bear. Despair and hopelessness saturated the atmosphere of my life.

I began to slowly feel like I was contributing to my partner's burden as a caregiver. It was a heartbreaking assemblage: a nefarious combination of feeling like a burden, the psychiatric symptoms of my disease and the inexplicable depression it aroused, and ongoing experiences of medical marginalization that conspired to push me further into the anarchic depths of despair. Eventually, experimental hyperthermia treatment at a clinic in Germany would help ease some of my symptoms and bring me out of the thickness of hopelessness, but that didn't happen until midway through autumn 2017, and the preceding two years had been especially trying. So, on a quiet morning at the end of summer, I tried to take my life.

· · · · ·

The following months were months of hardship. Kim managed to hold everyone and everything together, caring for Takoda and our two girls by herself, never once wavering in her support of me—she came to visit me every day I was in the psychiatric unit. I know that time was hard on her. The revelation that our relationships with others and the meanings we give to the world are vulnerable to collapse at any moment really shook her. But with persistence, courage, an open mind, and inimitable strength, she continued to care for me. She helped pull me through the dimness of my disease.

During this crisis, my experience of relational disability shifted to an intimate first-person perspective. It's hard to capture how these experiences alter us. From such depths of pain and suffering I learned how fragile life is in the throes of illness and the crucial parts we play in each other's lives, the importance of being recognized and listened to by others, and our need for connection. Through giving and now receiving care, I learned how inevitably dependent we are on each other. As Friedrich

Nietzsche recognized, "I doubt that such pain makes us 'better'; but I know that it makes us more profound."[41] The experience opened me up and deepened me in many ways. It gave me a new appreciation for those around me and enhanced my empathy and compassion for other people's suffering. A clarifying light was thrown on cultural idealizations of masculinity and the healthy body, forcing me to confront my demand for control and mastery (of myself and sometimes others), alongside my complicity in perpetuating unjust social arrangements through comporting with patriarchal masculine ideals and behaviors.

Perhaps most significantly of all, my feelings of social and self-alienation and experiences of medical mistreatment wrought by a complex and misunderstood illness, alongside those of being cared for by Kim, provoked critical reflection and improved the ways I cared for Takoda. I was able to map those feelings and experiences on to my interactions with him. I was reminded of how important presence, tactile gentleness, and open-mindedness are to giving care. I found myself less annoyed by the unpleasant aspects of care work, like changing his dirty diapers. Through caring and being cared for I learned to change my way of being with others. I believe nurturing these qualities will continue to make me a more attuned and responsive father, caregiver, and spouse.

· · · · ·

Our individual lives unfold within generalities of tradition that wield profound influence over our moral ways of being. The sketches throughout this chapter provide a view into the particulars of individuals' private lives and the cultural and social conditions in which these experiences accumulate. In the case of men, there is no way to talk about the practice of caregiving without contending with histories of gendered experience and norms of masculinity that help to establish the parameters within which experience unfolds and articulates itself as meaningful.

Parents depend upon embodied responses and skills rooted in their experiences as caregivers in meeting the demands of particular situations. Typically, individuals are drawn to respond and act in relation to how they have become attuned to the world and others through their situated, affective, and intersubjective experiences as caregivers. But in the process of creating habitable worlds for themselves and their children, there are also moments in caregivers' lives when troubling norms, inclinations, and practices that are no longer livable or compatible with one's circumstances bubble to the surface. These moments of moral breakdown arise when we are no longer able to interact with objects, people, and occasions in ways that were once habitual. They can be produced in and through tensions between identities, for instance, those of caregiver and father, as they are embodied within one and the same person. The breakdown arising from the conflicting demands generated by the coexistence of seemingly incompatible identities can be morally productive in shaking loose deeply rooted assumptions and understandings about oneself and the world.

On these occasions, we may find ourselves out of step with the habitual practices of others in the community, as previously unrecognized moral sentiments are thematized, reflected upon, and altered through our attunement to new moral concerns, as was the case with Earl when the male breadwinner ideal no longer fit his frame of reality. Moments of moral breakdown can enable a shift from a governing causality to a first-person causality, forcing one to step outside their everyday moral mode of attunement and reflect on norms and values that are ordinarily backgrounded and lived through as orienting features of our phenomenal worlds. Tension arises: someone responds to your child in a way that no longer feels compatible with your sense of fairness, like Doug's discomfort with his father's brand of patriarchal authority; or a situation arises that calls attention to a disposition that no longer feels livable, as we saw in the case of my conflict with my brother; or one must reconcile themselves with unexpected circumstances that threaten one's identity, as those who have suffered through illness know all too well.

Times of moral breakdown have the potential to make the familiar feel strange. They can give form to what is often vague and indeterminate, making explicit taken-for-granted assumptions and attitudes that guide our moral encounters with others and social gendered understandings of the self embodied in our ways of behaving toward others and things. The intensity of these moments can open possibilities for new ways of thinking and acting to be fed back into the way the world is patterned and felt. Indeed, the end of ethical action is to "once again dwell in the unreflective comfort of the familiar," as Zigon puts it.[42]

The hope is to work through these ethical dilemmas and become more responsive and attuned to the demands they make. When care is present as a subtext, these experiences of breakdown hold the promise to be morally productive in heightening fathers' sensitivity and strengthening their relationality to others, making them more responsible for their actions and identities as men. Indeed, the subversive potential of care habits can cultivate a sense of responsibility to others. In fact, it is quite striking how many of the fathers involved in my study have become aware of troubling norms and habitual tendencies through caregiving, demonstrating the latter's potential to heighten one's awareness of one's relation to structures of privilege and oppression that organize the local moral landscape, prompting changes to the way one relates to others and themselves.

Change is slow. But it was often through wanting to be better partners and caregivers that the men in this book took steps to establish more equitable relations with others. This does not mean that they declared themselves pro-feminists and supporters of women's equality. In fact, some men seemed oblivious to patriarchal structures and relations and how they are sustained. Instead, these steps toward change were more discreet, engendered and inhabited over time through personal experiences that connected masculine dominance and authority to the social debasement and neglect of their children. These sorts of insights can appear most clearly when experience lays bare the social devaluation of disabled bodies and one's own complicity in perpetuating oppressive norms involved in their diminution. Slowly, fathers' practical relatedness to the world shifts as they cast off those parts of themselves that are no longer livable. Fathers' lives, therefore, are not free of contradiction or ambiguity.

I want to sound a cautionary note and then raise what could be considered an important omission from my consideration of gender and relationality. First, the stories presented here allude to only some kinds of breakdown experiences that are part of a much larger continuum, ranging from mild perturbations to radical existential breakdowns. These times can be as perilous as they can be morally productive. The way one responds, reflects upon them, or alters one's moral disposition is contingent upon the social, personal, and spiritual resources one brings to bear in creating one's life as a caregiver. My second point has to do with the ethical and practical limitations of focusing on fathers' experiences of care, namely how fatherhood is relationally constructed with or against motherhood. Rather than focusing on how fathers get a sense of themselves in relation to a specific "what" (e.g., motherhood), I have focused on how men form a sense of themselves as fathers in relation to their histories, that is to say, in relation to whom. In this case, attending to relations between men and children or parents and men is as equally worthy of consideration as attending to relations between men and women—although I have touched briefly on how my sense of who and what I am as a father and man is connected to my relationship with Kim.

Finally, while moments of breakdown can highlight norms that govern our lives, change is not always easy in a world textured by others, especially among those who maintain normative practices by being oriented within them. Encounters with others can be deeply objectifying and alienating. What develops out of these encounters can also bring about changes of a more overt political kind.

Connectivities

It is uncanny, the circularities we insert ourselves into, the connectivities we get caught up in, the fragmentary moments we inhabit, that slip through our existential fingers, only to be reinhabited anew. And what of our adherence to things caught between what they are no longer and what they are yet to become?

The boy and his grandfather, Francis, are driving down remote backroads on their way to Nancy Martin's place. She's a recent widow and Francis likes to buy groceries and deliver them gratis. He does this for all the widows he mingles with on Friday nights at the Arthur Murray Dance Studio. The boy is licking a vanilla ice cream cone that his grandfather brought him moments ago from a nearby drugstore that will, decades later, become a Whole Foods Market. The boy watches the countryside passing by in a blur. He thinks of how someday he would like to be a famous ballroom dancer, someone like Arthur Murray himself. He doesn't know it now, but his dancing dreams will be crushed when he realizes that he can't memorize the dance steps. By comparison, he makes the heavy-footed cop and burly Irish guy taking the same class look like Anna Pavlova. It's this inability to memorize sequences that will cause him to fail chemistry. Instead, the boy will grow up and become a paramedic.

When he is nineteen years old, he will, one day, decide to miss the family's weekly dinner at Francis's home. On the night of his absence, death will surge up to meet Francis and it will be a heart attack that removes him from the world.

Frequently, Francis told the boy to marry a nice Jewish girl. To buy a house. To have kids. At first glance, it's as if Francis accomplished the impossible, like he ripped open the fabric of time and peered into the unfolding of things. But the future's contours would be different. The boy would marry a nice Jewish girl, who would later become an eminent professor in Romantic literature, but when their two children are diagnosed with the same rare genetic disorder, an unbridgeable chasm would claim the space between them, propelling them along different paths.

Francis stops at a red light and the boy licks the ice cream residue off his young, chubby fingers. A man crosses the road in front of them. His body is bent, and his stride is labored and unnatural. The stranger looks up long enough for the boy to see his face is twisted to one side. Francis gently grips the boy's thigh and says something the boy will remember long after his own children are diagnosed. He says: "And that's why we get our shots at the doctor's."

5 Belonging and Being-for-Others

The day had arrived for Randall and Kathy Stuart to meet their future daughter-in-law's parents. They didn't know too much about the Haddons, except that they were part of the Colorado country-club set. The Stuarts' son, Glen, had been dating Sally for four years, and Randall and Kathy had gotten to know her quite well during that time. To them, she was down-to-earth, easy to get along with, and possessed none of her parents' reported pretentious elitism. Ordinarily, Glen spent Christmas with his future in-laws in Colorado. But this year, because of their engagement, the Haddons had traveled over eight hundred miles south to spend Christmas with the Stuarts in their blue-collar neighborhood on the fringes of the Sonoran Desert. There was no other option anyway. Traveling with the Stuarts' daughter, Sam, required too much preparation and effort. And lately, with her kidney issues, Sam found travel especially tiring. Last year's trip upstate for her twenty-fifth birthday had left them all exhausted, culminating in Sam's frantic meltdown in the congested commuter traffic on the way home, where she directed her abject energy toward Kathy by mounting a physical attack.

At this time of year, the weather was temperate, and the desert evenings were cool. Kathy and Randall set up the outside patio, which opened onto big skies bounded by jagged mountain ranges, for dinner. Randall was happy that Sam was in a mild mood and seemed excited to have company. She was always more relaxed in her own dwelling, making it easier to manage things if anything unforeseen happened, which was unforeseeably predictable.

The evening had started like Randall anticipated: stiff and formal. But as the night wore on everyone increasingly eased into comfortable conversation. Randall glanced across the table and was both relieved and joyed to observe Glen engaged and unguarded. He knew how anxious Glen had been about them meeting his future in-laws. After all, growing up with Sam hadn't always been easy. The past was loaded with as many laments as triumphs. But tonight, Glen seemed happy, almost buoyant. Randall shifted his gaze to Sam; she glowed beatifically. When she was comfortable, her teasing and playful self—usually reserved for intimate others— could be glimpsed by everyone. Enjoying a new sense of ease, he thought tonight was one of those nights that offered a momentary reprieve, a balancing of the scales between the grind and joy of caregiving.

But halfway through an earnest conversation with Mr. Haddon, Randall felt a shift in the atmosphere. Then, Mr. Haddon's face turned pale and still as plaster. Randall turned his head toward the source of the disruption. It was Sam. She was standing before them, completely naked, gripping a wet diaper in her right hand. The Haddons shifted uneasily in their seats, glanced down at their watches, at anything to distract themselves. Randall felt the lived space between them thicken with a palpable incomprehensibility. Sally stifled a giggle and Glen collapsed back inside himself.

For Kathy and Randall, this was a common occurrence. Under normal circumstances one of them would usually gently rebuke Sam and usher her inside to be cleaned up and changed. But tonight was different. Tonight, there was an audience. Kathy and Randall exchanged a look brimming with shared awareness; an exchange that spoke to their shared history of caregiving. Kathy's expression of warmth and mutuality had the effect of allaying his anxieties. Slowly, he began to relax back into himself and thought, "You can dance around it for so long but here it is in living color. Welcome to our world."

. . . . .

When parents arrive into their worlds of disability they are faced with the demands of acquiring unfamiliar knowledge and skills in order to meet the complex needs of their children: developmental, medical, and psychosocial. At the time of my study, the men involved were caring for children ranging from five to twenty-six years of age. Their diagnoses varied—sensory, intellectual, and physical—as did their needs. Despite the variation in their embodied differences, however, they all required a high level of attention and vigilance. Income, time available, and support are all crucial factors for caregivers. At one time, Doug recalled both his boys receiving up to fifty hours a week of in-home therapies. Doug and Mary, his wife at the time, both worked second shifts. Doug returned from his full-time job in the evenings to care for the boys, while Mary headed off to university to work on her doctoral dissertation or teach classes. Availability and access to social services varies widely across the United States and accessing them can be time-consuming and bureaucratically cumbersome. Many of the parents in my study resided in Arizona and had received, or were receiving, disability support and services from the government, for example, in-home and habilitation services and/or respite through the Arizona Department of Economic Security (DES) and the Division of Developmental Disabilities (DDD).

Parents' new lives as caregivers are often colored radically differently from their previous ones, as they familiarize themselves with their child's treatment programs (speech therapy, occupational therapy, physiotherapy, applied behavioral analysis, nutrition services, for instance) and are thrust into medical spaces where suddenly partnerships with health care specialists take on new resonance. For many caregivers, a child's medical health care needs may require they obtain detailed knowledge on a range of medications and dietary related phenomena, or grow competent using various medical technologies, for instance, mechanical ventilators and gastrostomy tubes. Some parents relocate to areas that offer better support and services; others must seek housing that can accommodate wheelchairs and hospital beds and other essential equipment.

Parents' experiences with the educational system may also look different to how they expected as they find themselves dealing more regularly with school districts and school professionals to make sure their children are receiving appropriate accommodations. In the United States, the primary law protecting the rights of students with disabilities is the Individuals with Disabilities Education Act (IDEA), which requires that a child have an Individual Education Program (IEP) outlining their educational needs.[1] The additional educational-related matters that parents of children with disabilities face often require a heightened degree of parent-teacher interaction. It's in the best interest of one's child if parents familiarize themselves with the rules and regulations underpinning this educational contract to ensure that the primary tenets of IDEA—that a child is accessing their right to a Free and Appropriate Public Education (FAPE) in the Least Restrictive Environment (LRE) possible—are being upheld. At one time or another, these various activities and practices are constitutive of a socializing process for parents, as they learn how to navigate the new and diverse aspects of their everyday worlds.

The phenomenon of disability comes already shaped by the meanings and common-sense expectations with which parents grasp it. They simply form part of the situation. For instance, parents caring for children with disabilities are typically thrown into and participate in state and federally funded health care regimens rooted in a biomedical view of health and well-being, structured not only around a child's health care needs but around normalizing a child's identity and life through particular medical and therapeutic interventions. Early developmental habilitation programs, for example, are based on neurodevelopmental and behavioral outcomes oriented around changing, correcting, and improving communication styles, movements, eating patterns, emotional expressions, and behaviors.

Western cultural standards of bodily normality, our cultural orientation toward restitution, and modern medicine's desire to control and maintain bodies compel parents to feel, at least in the beginning, as though they must work toward training their children to achieve standards and behaviors that are as culturally normative as possible. Philosopher Susan Wendell underscores this point when she writes, "Our proximity to the standards of normality is an important aspect of our identity and our sense of social acceptability."[2] "Disciplines of normality," as she puts it, are "institutionally unbound ... internalized by most of us and socially pervasive."[3] They require us "to meet physical standards, to objectify our bodies, and to control them."[4] Indeed, they are the preconditions of participation in social life and are, as she puts it, "unnoticed by most adults who can conform to them without conscious effort."[5]

Years ago, a current affairs program called *Sunday Night* featured a father and his young son, who was born with quadriplegic cerebral palsy.[6] The story was framed around the medical profession's underestimations of a father's love and determination. An intense weekly schedule consisting of a variety of intensive therapies, orchestrated by the boy's devoted father, assisted the boy in "overcoming the odds" and standing for the first time. This milestone was followed by several more, with the boy eventually learning to walk and talk. Two years after the birth of my own son, this story (and its follow-up) had a substantial influence on my emotional experience as a father, as I received calls and advice from well-meaning family members who had watched the program, telling me of my son's potential and the possibilities born from patience and tenacity.

While this story captures a loving bond between a committed father and his vulnerable son, what troubles me most is how this story genre perpetuates a moral imperative to "fix" one's child and supports the idea that an individual's worth is contingent upon their degree of self-control and potential for social conformity. But, in a more immediate sense, it was emotionally painful and alienating. It made me feel that, by not adhering to this cultural script of "overcoming the odds," I was a failure and was failing my son. Stories like these presume a homogeneity not only of disability but of people's experiences surrounding it.

Perhaps one of the greatest challenges for parents is learning how to comfortably inhabit this space between things: between a world of language and a world of preverbal communication; between their meaning-rich perceptions of their children and the devaluating gaze of the other; between different and often incommensurate apprehensions of reality. Indeed, nothing is perhaps more painful than the growing awareness of your child's transgressions with reference to social norms and patterns of interaction (the piercing gazes and curious finger-pointing that come to enclose one's public life), or more important than carving out spaces of belonging for their equal moral treatment.

Merleau-Ponty's ideas on the relationality of embodied consciousness throw light on the lived body as the carrier of habits, which is useful in exploring the role dominant styles of being play in maintaining the orientation of the able-bodied community, as well as demonstrating that such bodily styles and perceptual orientations (so central to the maligning and diminishment of those with disabilities) may be refigured. Here

I continue unpacking the limitations and possibilities for how individual people experience a world made up of others. In doing so, I consider relational patterns and the sedimentation of shared cultural practices that define our sociocultural world and produce ableist contexts that mobilize the ubiquitous and devaluating gaze that assesses and devalues those with severe disabilities. In what follows, I draw from field notes to explore what it means for parents to navigate public spaces shaped by ableist perceptual practices and experience their children objectified in the other's gaze. These experiences do not only reveal how embodied subjectivity is shaped and constrained by sociocultural and structural forces. They also reveal the deeper layers of relationality between human beings.

BEING-FOR-OTHERS

Uncanny sensations can grip us in an instant, sometimes as terse and fleeting encounters. Other times, they linger in their passing, growing in virulence until their conspicuous features are given form.

Grim green lighting infuses the shadowy darkness of the room. Old, rusty wheelchairs adorn the ceiling. A stained mattress on a metal bedframe sits in the corner. Straightjackets are scattered with abandon. There's a man sitting on the floor, clad only in striped pyjamas, holding his knees. His face is a mask of neglect and abandon. He looks at me with a strange, grim expression. A figure appears before me, draped in a white nightgown, inky long black hair covering its face; something like Adako Yamamura from Koji Suzuki's *Ring* novel series. The silent figure lunges toward me. I narrowly circumvent its grasp. And then I am back outside in the warm night.

Below the surface of confusion there's a leadened recognition: some will always count more than others.

．　．　．　．　．

Takoda was four years old the first time I attended a Halloween haunted house attraction. The Celtic American tradition has not gained much traction in Australia. While we were staying in Scottsdale, Kim and I decided to get a babysitter and participate in the Halloween festivities. We attended a four-part outdoor haunt, one of the largest in the Valley. It was set amid a creepy twenty or so acres of cornfield. I enjoyed parts of the scarefest. But by the end of the night I was left with an overarching sense of unease. It was the wheelchairs, straightjackets, and imitation of mental patients inside the asylum haunt that threw me, evoking as they did some of North America's best-known mental hospitals and state facilities, where those with intellectual and developmental disabilities were routinely committed to an institutional life that was antitherapeutic, oppressive, and parasitic to their health and well-being.

In the asylum haunt, those with intellectual and developmental disabilities appear interchangeable with the likes of killer clowns and other demonic apparitions. They are represented as cultural objects of deviance, constructed purely on the grounds of objectification. The lived experiences of those once housed in dehumanizing settings are anonymized, their pain, suffering, and distress abstracted from their meaning context, denuded into a form of spooky entertainment. These representations create and perpetuate associations of cognitive disability with deviance and evil. Prejudices often underpin designations of insanity. Prejudices associated with cognitive disability are often channelled into the "creepy feeble-minded" or "mentally unstable" depictions witnessed in asylum haunts, and, I might add, the horror genre more broadly. What can be said about the fear and curiosity that the disabled figure evokes?

Philosopher and psychoanalyst Julia Kristeva suggests the disabled figure inflicts a threat of psychical or physical death.[7] The fear such a threat evokes is based on "the anxiety of seeing the very *borders of the human species* explode."[8] Therefore, she writes, "the disabled person is inevitably exposed to a discrimination that cannot be shared."[9] Similarly, philosopher Elizabeth Grosz says the disabled figure is constructed as an object of horror and fascination because differently embodied subjects imperil "the very definitions we rely on to classify humans, identities, and sexes—our most fundamental categories of self-definition and boundaries dividing self from otherness."[10]

It is not too much of an imaginative leap for me to picture Takoda in the not-too-distant past sitting in an overcrowded and understaffed institution amid the acrid smells of urine and lye, his soprano whine cutting through the sounds of weeping and wailing, rocking back and forth in distress. In fact, I feel most vulnerable and estranged from others when

Takoda is changed into a body-for-others, of which my shame and anger make me aware. I can deal with many of the new and unfamiliar activities and practices that have become an important part of my new world of disability, but this is different. That is because what others think of us and how they treat us matters in deep and nontrivial ways.

The popular appeal of haunted asylum attractions and the reductive portrayals they churn out speaks to a "common," or shared, sense of how the world works, which acts as a culturally constituted and culturally specific backdrop against which we make sense of the world, of ourselves and others.[11] The relevant point here is that common sense is not simply knowledge. Common sense enjoys near consensus, but it should not be understood as something that is imposed or deliberately taken up. Rather, these assumptions and feelings that guide our actions are preconscious, lived, embodied, expressed, and reproduced in our typical ways of experiencing things.

As Alcoff demonstrates in relation to race, while categorizations do sometimes operate on the basis of perceivable differences, perception also represents contextual knowledge that is often immune to reflection, sedimented into our psyches in a process that is reinforced each day.[12] Her point applies to corporeal diversity more generally, and thus dominant perceptions of disability as not entirely human, as frightful, as pitiful and/or tragic, as proximate to psychical or physical death are revealed to be the result of the plague and power of dominant perceptual orientations that affect our behavior and decision-making. Thus, perceptual practices not only determine what we see but the everyday situations we find ourselves in. The sedimentary nature of embodiment—those persistent perceptual, linguistic, and affective remnants informed by previous experience, politics, language, and history that become preconscious, practical knowledge of how to relate to and get along with others—deeply affect parents' experiences of caregiving as they move through different social settings with their children.

BEING AND THE BETWEEN

Merleau-Ponty's notion of syncretic sociability, that is, a subject's interconnectedness with the social world and others is helpful here. He describes this as the "mutual impingement of the other and myself at the heart of a situation."[13] The intertwining of self and other that he identifies means that our style of being in the world (perceptions, selfhood, patterns of thought, introceptive sense, posture, and ways of moving) is formed in and through our interactions with others in a sociohistorical world. As Rosalyn Diprose phrases it, "Just as through the look and the touch of the other's body I feel my difference, it is from the same body that I borrow my habits and hence my identity without either body being reducible to the other or to itself."[14] Thus, we find our style of being shaped in and through those around us in a common historical world. What does this mean for parents who undergo changes to their style of being-in-the-world, effected in and through caregiving, which leads to seeing, living, loving, and relating to others in new ways? I suggest we think of parents as between things, as travelers between conflicting apprehensions of reality.

While a subject's style of being in the world is fluid to a degree, sedimentation ensures that some stability and a felt constancy of subjectivity across time are engendered in and through remnants of a person's past and prior comportment. Many of the men I spent time with admitted to their own ignorance or negative attitudes toward disability growing up. This goes some way in explaining the conditions under which parents find themselves feeling so existentially adrift from others upon entering their worlds of disability. The structural dimension of our bodily relation to others underwrites parents' experience of existential disruption: a profound sense of estrangement arises from one's departure from the normative sequence of major life events and through a consideration of the standpoints and perspectives of others.

From this double life parents live arise situations of exposure to the views of others, namely, when their children become a body-for-others. In these situations, parents fall out of coherence with their social surroundings as they experience their children seized in the scrutinizing or objectifying gaze of other people, their corporeality coming into acute self-awareness. In what follows, I bring into focus the role negative self-conscious emotions play in parents' experiences of disability and caregiving, and the alteration to experience brought about by moments of disclosure and rejection linked to the views of others, particularly in experiences of shame. My use of the term shame encompasses a variety of cognate emotions related to the other's gaze, including mortification and social discomfort. These emotive responses are elicited in parents insofar as they actively belong to a sociohistorical world from which taken-for-granted, ableist practices spring forth. And yet they are deeply aware of the practices that diminish the humanity of children with disabilities. A problem parents face, then, is how to go about transcending these painful situations and carving out spaces of belonging where their children might be experienced otherwise.

PAUL AND PEARL

I had been reading Paul's online blog for a couple of years before I contacted him to be a part of my research. His virtual self was articulate, assertive, cognitively agile, and, at times, downright intimidating. He projected himself online as a voracious advocate for his daughter, Pearl, and documented with detail and caustic humor his charged encounters with medical and educational professionals, alongside his troubles and successes navigating the web of bureaucratic processes caregivers find themselves caught up in as they attempt to secure support and resources for their children—and which permeate civil life more broadly. With unsurpassed temerity, he wrote candidly about his strengths and shortcomings and, I think, by not pretending to be more than he was, he drew a strong online following.

On a Tuesday in August I arrived in Boston to meet Paul. The warm air was thick with a sticky humidity that abetted the fatigue-induced nausea sitting defiantly in my stomach. I had arrived six hours earlier on a red eye from Phoenix and had only managed a couple of hours sleep. After several minutes of waiting outside my Airbnb, a four-story walk-up townhouse just down the road from Brookline Village, Paul arrived. I climbed into the car and was immediately struck by his long and slender frame. He was a lot taller than I imagined: around six feet four. He was wearing pants and a dark polo shirt featuring the logo of his now defunct high-tech computer engineering business.

We shook hands and he pulled back onto the road, heading toward Brookline Village.

"How are things? How was the flight?" he asked in a slow and melodious Boston drawl, that would, over time, insinuatingly worm its way into my memory.

"Good. Hey, thanks for picking me up."

"You want to get something to eat or a coffee?"

"Coffee sounds great," I replied.

"Then we can head back to my place and you can meet Alice. The girls will be home later so you can meet them then."

Paul's life had changed significantly over the last year. His online identity cohered around his status as a single dad and the experiences involved in intense caregiving for his profoundly disabled daughter. He unapologetically documented the ambivalences and ambiguities he felt about caregiving. Blogging served as an accommodating platform. Through writing he could articulate issues and concerns that he didn't always feel comfortable sharing with people in person. As an older male tending to a vulnerable female body, cultural incest taboos were an irritating feature of his everyday social interactions. In fact, I was initially drawn to his blog because it threw light on this often-unrecognized situation and relationship between father and daughter. I found it interesting that he was subverting this taboo system through necessity.

During our time together, many of his recollections spoke to the heavy burden of being vulnerable to the distortions of others.

"I've had it in changing rooms," he tells me, "when Pearl was smaller and I wanted to change her or try clothes on and they [sales assistant] would ask, who's going to help her? My own sister, a very intelligent and loving lady, said to me, shouldn't you get someone to bathe and dress her in the morning?" He feigns dismay. "She's never had a kid of her own," he concludes, seemingly excusing her ignorance as naivete. "I said to her, if I'm with mom and she's having real trouble getting in and out of the bathtub, is it OK if I help her? She said, yeah, of course. So, it's an ingrained thing."

He also recounted interactions with medical professionals and mandated reporters. There was an incident when Pearl was much younger, for example, when a school nurse called Paul to notify him that she had put up an ad for someone to help him with bathing and dressing her in the morning. He was flabbergasted. He didn't ask her for help. He didn't need it. During their phone conversation the catalyst that prompted her interference came to light: earlier that week she had checked Pearl's diaper and discovered that she was not as clean as she thought she should have been. He was overwhelmed by her accusation of neglect. He wasted no time explaining to her that Pearl lives in a diaper 24/7 and always experiences discharge before menstruation. "Do you have any clue what her care at home is?"

It was unclear whether the nurse was acting in response to legislative requirements to report suspected cases of child neglect—failure to do so is often punishable by a fine or court action—or some other whim. Regardless, he had the matter resolved by lodging a complaint with the school district superintendent's office. "I also passed on a fact that no one else in the school district knew," he tells me, "that my girlfriend at the time was living with us and was nurse manager at a pediatric rehabilitation hospital." He recalled getting a phone call a couple of days later with an explanation, "not an apology: the nurse had a problem with a single father taking care of teenage girl."

We entered a café in Brookline Village and took a seat at an empty table toward the back. It was a busy place, with scuffed hardwood floors and light mahogany accents. Customers were eating to a background of '80s music. During breakfast he told me the blog wasn't for everyone—hence the use of a pseudonym. When I asked him if his sister or mother ever read it, he replied, "I don't need to have my mother, Pearl's loving grandmother, reading some of those things. I don't know if you understand this *yet* but very few people understand."

Within the blogosphere, Paul's views were accepted and encouraged, and he liberally omitted anything outside the purview of his experiences with Pearl. It wasn't surprising, then, when I found out that he'd stopped blogging once his situation changed. The blog's entire premise no longer worked. Just twelve months earlier his household population expanded from two to four.

Alice was in her mid-fifties. She was small in stature but big in intellect. She met Paul within the blogosphere, where she also wrote about her experiences mothering Ava, her severely disabled daughter who was roughly the same age as Pearl. After a whirlwind courtship, they were married, and Alice and Ava emigrated from Canada to live with Paul and Pearl in Massachusetts. Paul recalled the event that precipitated his decision to propose to Alice.

The day had started off like any other, with Paul sending Pearl off on the school bus, "with full trust and total fear as usual," he recalled. Indeed, it's a fear that any parent can relate to and one that is inevitably deepened when a child is incomparably dependent on the good will of others—especially when this good will has historically been in short supply. When she returned home from school her eye was partially swollen shut, her bra was on backward, and, later, he discovered a cut on her vulva. He questioned the teachers, but nobody could explain why her bra had been repositioned or why her eye was swollen. A full investigation ensued.

Perhaps the most frustrating and damning thing is that Pearl, like Takoda, inhabits a preverbal world. Without the expressive capacity of language, children like ours can't bear witness to the failures and inhuman misdeeds of others—and even when they can, their testimony is often institutionally discredited, for these are anomalous bodies that are socially tainted with a damaged subjectivity.

Three months after he recognized Pearl had been sexually assaulted, they were attending a doctor's appointment together. Paul raised her assault in conversation with the doctor and Pearl unexpectedly burst into tears, affirming what he had known all along. Back home, he locked himself in the bathroom and cried, his mind traveling toward all the things that had transpired and all that he was helpless to remedy. "You're supposed to protect your daughter," he told me. "You're supposed to fight for her and make sure she has every tool needed to become the best she can. You teach her love by example. I failed my daughter."

I suspect he said the same things to Alice over the phone in the bathroom that afternoon. He said Alice yelled at him, "Go and talk to your daughter. I don't care if she understands you or not. Go and talk to her and apologize." That night, Paul would lift Pearl, now a grown woman, from her wheelchair and would lie down on the bed next to her like they used to when her body was much smaller. He spoke to her for a couple of hours, made her promises, and told her he would visit school every single day, and then they abandoned themselves to a quiescent state of sleep. Paul knew, then, that he wanted to marry Alice.

For Paul, the above event is connected to a web of moments that have threatened Pearl with erasure.

When Pearl was fifteen, he got into a battle with the state of Massachusetts in an effort to exempt her from participating in standardized testing designed to track the progress of students.[15] He contacted state authorities, alerted the media, and petitioned the state commissioner of education, writing: "Pearl will experience heightened stress and anxiety at the time of the exam by not being physically able to respond to any part of the exam. She will experience loss of self-esteem and self-image by completely and totally failing an exam that is not designed to test or assess her knowledge but the mastery of the Massachusetts curriculum frameworks."

Paul also told me of other times Pearl's humanity was degraded, , like during seemingly benign and harmless procedural requirements, such as applying for Supplemental Security Income (SSI).[16] He was astounded by the volume of information and paperwork that was needed to meet eligibility requirements. Beyond the scheduled phone calls, paperwork, and state certificates certifying Pearl's disabilities, it was the *function report* that really got to him. In bold and all caps, he recalled, the document stated: DO NOT LEAVE ANSWERS BLANK. He explained that despite having all the documentation outlining her diagnosis, doctors' names, medications, etc., here was another eight-page document centralized around her physical and cognitive limitations. There was no space, he recalled, for preserving the things that make Pearl who she is. He was angry that there was no option for skipping the series of repetitious and unnecessary questions that he had answered elsewhere, and which didn't apply to Pearl's existence anyway. "She has a major effect on people, but you see none of that [in the report]," he said. It was the little things, according to Paul, that muted and supressed the hard realization that Pearl was profoundly disabled: "her contagious smile, her unexpected but well-timed bursts of laughter, and her snarky expressions."

On a Friday night, a few days into my second stay in Boston, he comes home late from work. In a vain attempt to escape the searing pain in his feet and back he collapses onto the kitchen floor. He doesn't look comfortable: he is half sitting, half lying on the floor, his long legs sprawled out before him, his back to the cabinets below the kitchen sink. He has spent the entire day in advocacy meetings. Ever since Pearl aged out of the school system a couple of years ago he has directed his efforts to building a career as a special education advocate and special education surrogate parent—putting to use the advocacy experience and expertise he acquired throughout his years navigating the special education system for Pearl.[17]

"I used to wrestle with this one," he says. "If they gave me a pill and said give this to Pearl and she will be normal, here's the cure, would I give it to her?" He reflects for a moment: "I'd lose Pearl. But how do you define Pearl? If I gave Pearl a pill and she wakes up in the morning and says, 'fuck you, daddy. I'm getting my nipples pierced,' would I give her the pill? The conclusion I come to is"—he pauses, and his face assumes an expression that evokes in me a mix of melancholy and an ineffable knowing that reaches down deep in my heart—"probably." Then, in a flat voice: "I would lose my Pearl." He pauses. "But I always look at quality of life from her point of view. So, can I give her half a pill and then she'll be able to tell me if she wants it? I don't know. Pearl is all I know. Pearl is what I have."

The following day, a cold and overcast afternoon, we are driving to Natick, a suburb just outside Boston. There's a durable medical equipment (DME) supplier that Paul goes to when Pearl's wheelchair needs repairs or servicing. "People are not empathetic," he says. I nod as if I understand. "We have a great team of doctors, teachers, and therapists," he continues, "but there have been...there was a doctor and he wanted me to lift up her shirt so he could see her development and he never even got off his chair. He never spoke directly to her. And he wanted *me* to just lift up Pearl's shirt so he could see her development. I said, 'I have a better idea.' And I opened the door and walked out. Show some respect on some level. That was really awful."

I look out the window. There's an old homeless-looking guy splayed out on a bench, and a couple talking nearby, perhaps in their early thirties; the woman is holding a baby. Far in the distance an ambulance siren warbles. Everywhere I look there are traces of things happening.

"They don't put themselves in other people's positions," Paul says. "Pearl loves swimming. That's something we know she really loves. There was a school swimming day and the regular PT was absent. They [teachers] found out a little late and so they still changed Pearl into her bathing suit and had her sit by the pool, *not go in*, and at the end of the hour changed her back into her clothes and put her back in the classroom. I said, OK, and did someone *explain* to Pearl why she had to watch everyone else do exactly what she loves and wasn't allowed? Did someone ever think that maybe that wouldn't be so nice to her? Could you have called me, so I could have come down to the pool and gone in with her myself? Could you have kept her in the classroom? Could you have done anything else? Did anyone look at it from her point of view? No. Empathy: thinking of things from other people's point of view. It's a big deal."

My mind wanders. I recall an event a couple of years ago when Takoda was two. I took him with me to the post office in town. As we waited in a long, crowded line he clamped his hands down over his ears and broke into a lengthy, soprano scream. A woman glanced back at us, twisted her face in disgust, clicked her tongue, and then clamped her hands over her own ears. My face flushed red, exuding heat. I felt strangled. My limbs felt heavy. I was angry and embarrassed. One awkward moment seemed to pile on top of the other until she was finally served and made her undignified exit. I was reeling with confusion over her reaction. I couldn't think clearly. I didn't know how to respond.

Author Michael Lewis says that one of the primary features of shame is intense discomfort and anger.[18] Check! Another feature he identifies is feeling that one is unworthy. Check! Although in my case it was a feeling that my son was unworthy, a kind of shame by association. In shame, Lewis also says we become the object and subject of shame: "the self system is caught in a bind in which the ability to act or to continue acting becomes extremely difficult."[19] The function of shame, then? According to Lewis, it is "to signal the avoidance of behaviors likely to cause it."[20] Shame functions to interrupt any action that violates internally or externally derived norms or rules.[21] "The internal command," Lewis writes, "says, 'Stop. What you are doing violates a rule or a standard.'"[22]

In one sense, then, shame is an important part of human experience. It checks the flow of our interactions and works to maintain a coherent and stable moral and social world. But experiences of shame can also be profoundly restricting, a serious obstacle to achieving fulfillment, recognition, and dignity.

Like many of Paul's experiences, my own with the woman at the post office provides a window into ableist attitudes and behaviors that serve to enforce norms of public behavior and create and maintain the spatial boundaries of the able-bodied community. Sadly, when we fail to grasp the intentions of another or become empathetically unavailable, as this woman clearly was, the mutual recognition necessary for the confirmation of moral worth is lost. Jean-Paul Sartre's analysis of shame gives us insight into the experience of alienation that throws the subject back upon himself or herself and the ongoing effects these experiences have on the lives of parents undergoing them.

According to Sartre, "the look" of the "other" during an encounter confers the relation of Being-seen-by-another, whereby "I experience the revelation of my being-as-object."[23] To this end, when parents feel self-conscious about their children's behavior or comportment, or appraise their situations as they are surely to be appraised by others, it is as a body experienced in this mode of dispossession. One's consciousness and the world it organizes thus undergo an alienating destruction by virtue of the other's critical gaze.[24] The experience of disapproval or rejection engenders a heightened awareness of the self. When parents feel caught up in the look of the other, their meaning-rich perceptions of their children are threatened as the situation organizes itself around the other's perspective and understanding.[25] In this sense, when parents feel like their child's behaviors and expressions are not understood, they are forced to view themselves and their children as others see them, observed as objects stripped of subjectivity. It is this disruption to pre-reflective bodily experience and movement of life, experienced with a feeling of self-devaluation, that gives rise to self-conscious emotions like shame. Therefore, shame can be understood as a distinct form of self-perception from the standpoint of others, or members of a social community.

Because shame is often bound to the presence of others it can be a fleeting experience for some. However, for some parents of severely disabled children, though certainly not all, the experience of shame can take on a more chronic state, which pervades their lives. The omnipresent pressures for one's child to conform to seemingly obvious social rules and values can induce a binding self-consciousness, especially when one continually anticipates disapproval, fully aware that one's child will fail against these standards—for example, a child may have a meltdown in a supermarket and elicit judgemental stares from strangers for being disruptive, or parents may witness strangers openly staring or turning away in disgust at their child's behavior in a restaurant because they are making strange noises or eating with their mouth open. This can strike open a chasm between self and others that cannot be easily bridged. For many parents, this may effectively ensure they avoid public spaces with their children.

Interpersonal spaces can grow increasingly threatening as the restricting and individualizing effects of shame gain a pervasive power. Consequently, the corporeal normativity of care-less spaces goes unchallenged. There was a brief time when I felt like I could no longer pass through the world with Takoda without a reproachful glance, without feeling this mysterious and painful disturbance of lived time. I began to wonder more and more about how parents bypass or overcome these situations on their way to finding some kind of "normal."

I didn't bother sharing my story with Paul, I'm not sure why; nor did I tell him that the woman's actions had the desired effect of making me feel uncomfortable and incredibly anxious about running errands with Takoda in the future. The more I thought about this moment, and others just like it, the more I wished I had Paul's ability to immediately respond to the demands of these interpersonal situations and do what works in Takoda's best interest. It wasn't only his ability to arrive at the best strategy required to intervene at the level of law and policy that I envied, it was his spontaneity in ethical action, that is, his ability to act intuitively without detaching himself from the concrete situation.[26]

Things do not go well at the DME. When we pick up Pearl's wheelchair from the supplier, Paul notices that the laterals have been repositioned incorrectly. Earlier that morning, Paul was emphatic that he didn't want them messing around with the laterals because Pearl's physical therapist had carefully set and positioned them while looking at X-rays showing Pearl's scoliosis. He even took pictures beforehand of their placement as a safeguard. The technician denied touching them. And a flush of anger had turned him scarlet at Paul's insistence that he was in the wrong.

"I can't believe they fucked up," Paul says, as we drive back to Brookline with Pearl's broken chair in the back.

"You knew they would."

"Welcome to the world of assholes."

There's a long silence. We merge on to the empty freeway. It's late and the sun is starting to lose some of its force.

"If this was some other piece of equipment would you care as much?" I ask, finally breaking the silence.

"No. How dare you do this to Pearl. I mean, this is what they do to all of us as parents. This is all she has. This is her only *anything*. She could love the chair more than she loves me. OK. You don't do this. You *don't* do this to her."

"Why do you think they're so unhelpful?"

"That's a good question," he says. " I guess because no one holds them accountable. I don't know. I don't understand it. Is it an attitude that's just for cripples? Now we get into empathy. Some people have very low empathy. That's how you find people who matter in the world—I'm very convinced of that in my life. The difference between schmucks and everybody else is empathy. They can't empathize with Pearl. OK. You give them a kid in a chair and say go live for a week, then they'll learn a lot. They just don't empathize. They don't understand, you know. What's the big deal? They don't understand that life is tough enough, why are you adding to it? And again, would a car dealership give you a brand-new car with scratches on it? And would you take it? No. But I'm supposed to take a seven-thousand-dollar wheelchair with scratches on it? It just boggles my mind. It's just so infuriating and it's just that much worse because it's Pearl."

Later that night Paul sends me a copy of his email to the director of branch services and the rehab technology specialist. He opens the email by identifying the problem with the laterals and the obstinacy of the technicians. Then he writes: "So, in brief (!) the laterals need to be fixed, the seat cover needs to be replaced, the abductor wedge needs to be replaced and *Pearl deserves an apology*."

BEING DRAWN INTO CARE

In this chapter I have spent time moving through various situations wherein parents' thinking becomes introverted and oriented around the body and selfhood of their children. By describing these events, I have tried to reveal their ubiquitous nature in the lives of parents of children with disabilities. The source of shame can be internal or external, felt publicly or privately. These experiences of shame underscore Merleau-Ponty's point that the distinction between self and other is not absolute.[27] Our presence in the world is a co-presence, because the other's emotional presence is a fundamental constituent of our lifeworld's dynamic, often grasped through the body.

As we have seen, the experience of shame and others like it presuppose our ability to see ourselves as others do. While they can play a regulating role in the interpersonal sphere, they can also motivate a deterioration of syncretic sociability, collapsing the interpersonal bridge between self and other. This interpersonal uncoupling can lead to feelings of estrangement and social phobia. In the last analysis, shame reveals our deeper layers of relationality and our need for social belonging.

Some thinkers posit that an elementary feeling of shame, as an affect, is present in infancy, arising from a mismatch between an infant's expectations and the response from others and the environment, "a painful emotion responding to a sense of failure to attain some ideal state," as philosopher Martha Nussbaum writes.[28] In infancy an elementary feeling of shame arises from an awareness of separation from others; indeed, babies demonstrate a responsiveness to others in a way that shows an innate capacity for shared action and experience through precommunicative sympathy or syncretic sociability. For example, experiments like the "blank face test" demonstrate that infants quickly become distressed when mothers stop communicating with them and adopt a blank face.[29] Initially, babies appeal for communication by gesturing and vocalizing. When their attempts to reestablish a connection fail, infants quickly become distressed and unhappy, displaying all the bodily behavior correlative with the kind of self-conscious behavior expressed by adults in a state of shame.[30]

Developmental researchers Colwyn Trevarthen and Kenneth J. Aitken suggest that relational emotions, like elementary shame, are "fundamental to human consciousness," contribute to the building of "relationships of affectionate attachment," and are "primary and necessary to the child's entry into the social/cultural world . . . with all the conventions and rituals that world offers."[31] Similarly, philosopher Heidi Maibom suggests that human shame is an "implicit acknowledgement of a demand to live in accordance with public norms and standards."[32] In short, our experiences of shame in later life, where our concern for social norms drives our desire to form and maintain relationships with others and create sense of belonging, have their foundations in these early experiences of shame, which are deeply grounded in our vulnerability and connectedness to one another. As author Hugh Mackay writes, as social and communal beings "we are defined... and sustained by our social networks. We thrive on being part of a community."[33]

It might be said that the way society has historically identified people with disability as being socially inadequate, and their systemic expulsion from everyday spaces of activity and belonging, has worked to attenuate our respect and tolerance, while creating and maintaining the boundaries of the able-bodied community. Therefore, the misunderstanding and measure of carelessness evident in the situations I have described might seem like a foregone conclusion. However, the historical givenness of life and background biases and understandings we bring to our encounters with others are not the sum total of meaning making. People are not determined by history. They make history through actions. Experiences and events happen over time, and so does the flow of meaning. While it is true that we come to each situation oriented by the way we are attuned to perceive things, against a background of shared habits and customs that affect the kinds of experiences we have access to, we are not destined to deal with things in a specific fashion. Sometimes understanding others involves an encounter that leads to personal or social change.

Social change was the hope of some of the fathers I spent time with. I started to see these moments of shame and social discomfort as windows into the springs and motives that propel parents in their individual and collective attempts to challenge and transform spaces of social activity and belonging. Many of the fathers remarked on how they tried to trouble or alter the perceptions, experiences, and thinking of others. For example, Earl told me that when he notices people doggedly staring at Zachary, whether with seeming curiosity or disapproval, he candidly comments on Zachary's nonverbal behavior and what it means. He hopes that by overtly addressing the looks he can deepen the way people experience Zachary and themselves. People often respond favorably, he said, dropping their guard and entering into conversation with him.

The importance of proximity, then, between nondisabled and disabled persons cannot be overstated. For as the scholar Sara Ahmed writes, "The stranger reappears as the one who is always lurking in the shadows."[34] Spaces of proximity offer sites of possibility to engage intersectional differences and rework the sedimented orientations of others, subverting the divisions that organize social and political space. It can be hard to tell what effect the work done as part of parents' advocacy efforts has in the world. Changes in life happen slowly, in the play of intersubjective relations and communicative practice. Change operates in the tensions and tugs of tradition and revolt, between our freedoms and the determinations of the past that precedes us. At the level of everyday activism, Paul and Earl can be seen trying to realign the perceptions and thinking of others to foster the kind of attitudes and behaviors that grant embodied difference, trying to refigure interpersonal spaces through expressions of care and new layers of meaning through action.

Importantly, experiences of shame can become a springboard for moral development as parents develop expertise in caring through the new and different situations revealed to them in their everyday engagements with others vis-à-vis their children. What I came to understand—slowly and painfully over the ensuing years—is that these experiences of shame can lose their damning weight after a while as parents develop their ability to carefully feel their way through them. As Dreyfus puts it, "As ethical skills increase one would expect the expert to encounter fewer and fewer breakdowns."[35] This was certainly the case for Paul. His movements and behaviors in the throes of affect-laden experiences are spontaneous and automatic; to all appearances he certainly is quite devoid of the paralysis I had experienced in the post office and that had robbed me of the capacity for creatively engaging others. Being between realities can provide parents with the possibility of understanding multiple perspectives with the view of reconciling them. Paul showed me that being drawn into these calls for advocacy is a spiritual exercise: one's efforts have to be carried out in the spirit of what one is fighting for (accommodation and respect for our equal value), for the two cannot be separated without doing great damage to the truth.

Dreyfus suggests that experts in moral action are guided by intuition, rather than detached deliberation.[36] Experts, through vast experience, acquire the know-how to apply their skills and respond to ethical situations spontaneously, drawing on a repertoire of accumulated embodied responses and tactics.[37] Indeed, after navigating the changing and complex landscape of involved caregiving for over twenty years with and for

Pearl, Paul has developed an expertise in situational caring. He is not only sensitive to conditions of improvement but knows how to implement the right actions. He has developed a form of moral maturity characterized by his adeptness at perceiving Pearl's needs and vulnerabilities, a deepened commitment to ensuring she is treated equally by others, and knowledge on how to implement an action plan. In his development into an expert, Paul continually moves between advocacy that is intuitive and situational—acting effortlessly and intervening courageously for the welfare of his daughter—and the kind of advocacy that requires detached reasoning in order to intervene at the level of law and policy.

These situations are not inconsequential. The moral wisdom that informs Paul's actions makes available to the imaginations of others Pearl's embodied subjectivity and the realities of their life together. To act differently from the status quo in these situations begins a reversal of "the untold labor that goes into the sustaining and upkeep of identity," to borrow the words of author Anat Pick.[38] It is here, in these everyday social and affective spaces, that we see care as a background upon which situations and persons show up; a way of being attuned to what matters in the world through the skills of receptivity and openness.

6 The Axiom of Equality

"Welcome to Holland" is a widely distributed story, frequently given to and shared among parents of children with disabilities. It was first given to us by a service coordinator from Vision Australia, who provided the earliest of early intervention services for Takoda before we were properly integrated into social services. Emily Perl Kingsley, a social activist and mother of a son with Down syndrome, wrote the parable in 1987. The narrative depicts the initial disappointment of arriving to an unfamiliar destination (one's world of disability) through the metaphor of an unexpected journey to Holland instead of one's eagerly anticipated vacation to Italy. The story invites those who identify with it to enjoy the lovely things Holland has to offer (like its windmills and tulips) by discarding their expectations and recognizing Holland's possibilities, instead of mourning the loss of Italy's. While directed primarily at parents who may recognize themselves as having a shared experience, it works as an allegory for anyone grappling with the uncertainties of a new situation.

"Welcome to Holland" provides a counternarrative that resists reductive and dehumanizing cultural narratives that portray having a child with disabilities as a tragedy or, as folklorist Amy Shuman writes, "medical and social narratives about the child as an unwelcome problem."[1] When these counternarratives are authored by those with disabilities or their family members, they can be an important form of activism. Out of these counternarratives emerge rescriptings of disability and normalcy. As anthropologists Rayna Rapp and Faye Ginsburg point out, over the last fifty years a variety of cultural productions in North America (films, family memoirs, internet discussion groups, talk shows, etc.) have enabled families of children with disabilities to disseminate important insights about living life with disability to wider publics, "expanding the social fund of knowledge about disability."[2] These efforts, they suggest, broaden our understanding of kinship and relatedness beyond the scope of biological family to the realm of public culture.[3]

Admittedly, I was moved the first time I read Kingsley's essay. I found comfort in thinking I was a part of a new kinship network comprising families who had undergone similar experiences. Early on, I felt like her allegory represented and authenticated my experience of entering an unfamiliar world. But Shuman makes a good point when she suggests the parable erases "the difference that makes a difference in understanding others."[4] "Welcome to Holland," she suggests, attempts to align parents of disabled children by encouraging them to recognize Holland as "slower paced" than Italy and the disabled child as a "lost dream."[5] Slower paced isn't just different, she pointedly remarks, but "grounds for exclusion in many social worlds."[6] She offers this important insight in relation to her own experiences mothering a child with disabilities : "[W]hat is destabilizing... is not the loss of a dream but the loss of what I knew, what I took for granted."[7]

During fieldwork for this book, I reckoned with diverging and sometimes contradictory worldviews and interpretations of disability both within and across individuals, uncovering multiple converging and conflicting interpretations of life with disability that affect the ways parents feel positioned in relation to each other. One of the biggest difficulties of moral life is that it is limited by the conditions of our existence (historical, cultural, geographical, psychological, empirical, and practical). Moral experience is guided by the past and one's familiarity with the world. Conflicting agendas and definitions of the good can make caregivers' moral experiences fraught with uncertainties and difficulties. But subjectivity is also interpretive and intersubjectively embedded and, therefore, emergent. It is our existential limits and the fundamental interpersonal character of life that make questioning and new discoveries possible, exemplified by parents who cultivate a direct relational connection with their children and step into an intersubjective space where they coexist with them. This is what philosopher Martin Buber would call an I-Thou relationship.[8] In the I-It relationship, we treat people as things, according to Buber. However, when we stand in the I-Thou relationship we *encounter* the other.[9] The I-Thou stance is characterized by mutuality, not self-regard.[10] The nourishing experiences of human life can be found in this between space, in our encounters with other persons. As he puts it, "all real living is meeting."[11]

Parents' embodied intersubjective experiences of disability and caregiving can not only open up new ways of seeing things, obliging them to see the fundamental vulnerability we all share and our responsibility for each other, but can also give voice to what suffers inside them and in others, throwing into relief the urgency of their concerns and what matters in life. Their experience of disorientation and what transpires between them and their children in the context of giving care, then, can be the best teachers in moving them toward what is important for flourishing in their emotional and practical lives as caregivers. The presence of care can be an effective force in living out the values of openness, receptivity, and engagement, deepening our sense of self in its dependency on others and subverting those definitional differences with which we carve out niches of belonging and not belonging. The shared experience of caregiving can bring parents together through the familiar tremors of uncertainty and a shared inclusive ethos, as they try and shift reality from the I-It toward the I-Thou.

In the following account, I use creative nonfiction to represent a day in the life of Raul, a retired father who is the primary caregiver for his disabled daughter, Abigail. Embedded within this story are discussions of race, class, and income and how they figure into issues around community participation and access to health and care services. My explicit focus, however, is on the ways cargivers' subjectivities and ethical commitments take shape around the moral sentiments and intuitions that are formative for their identities. Here faith is shown to be a powerful moral source that articulates the moral field and what is given in experience. Moreover, Raul can be seen to draw on his faith in facing existential questions and making sense of his life. His religious and ethical orientation not only direct his ethical comportment toward the world and others but also underwrite his higher order ethical commitments and judgements.

Formulating a Heideggerian-inspired ethics, philosopher Lawrence Hatab uses the compound expression "ethically-being-in-the-world" to stand for the way we are situated and socialized beings already shaped by ethics before we reflect on it.[12] I feel comfortable using Hatab's notion that we are ethically thrown, that is, that meaningfulness is mediated by our own perspective while unfolding in an environment wider than myself and within terms of meaningfulness that are given to us, because it speaks to the ways our deeply held moral intuitions move and alter themselves as they are drawn into the "dynamic integration of past, present, and self."[13] Thus, moral action involves both new initiatives and habitual responses. As we will see, fathers' unconscious predispositions aid them in negotiating and expanding the boundaries of their world, announcing themselves in their moral commitments, the ways they respond to situations, and how they evaluate their lives according to what they feel is fair or unfair. Our diverse and constantly changing life situations and relationships with others, which are materially, affectively, and socially distinct, stir consciousness toward its various ethical possibilities and direct our ways of thinking, acting, and ethically being-in-the-world. Focusing on the disagreements and conflicts that emerge in moral life highlights the existential significance of caregiving amid difficulty and uncertainty.

Perhaps most importantly, though, I want to throw light on the relational lifeworlds of disabled children and their embodied moral interactions with others by attending to the bodily and emotional dimensions of their social lives. In what follows, I focus on modes of agency that are sometimes overlooked in our language-centered culture and forms of ethical life, and which are grounded in our capacities beyond rationality and autonomy.

BIGSBY STREET

Raul enjoyed spending his downtime watching others, usually from the corner table inside his favorite Subway restaurant. Sometimes he would visit the shopping mall and wander around watching other people talk and laugh, striking up a basic conversation with strangers, momentarily rejoining the outside world. Today was especially hot though, even for Phoenix, so he took refuge in the sandwich shop, absorbing the air-conditioned surroundings and filling himself with a tuna melt and cold soda. It had been over twelve years since Abigail was born and even though he had grown familiar with his life of caregiving, which was both temporally and geographically distant from his former one, every once in a while he missed the ease and indifference with which he had participated in his former social activities, which self-evidently satisfied his gregarious instincts.

In the past, he had been ambitious and avidly sociable. He grew up in a large Hispanic family in Bisbee, Arizona, a mining town in the Mule mountains, approximately eleven miles from the Mexican border. Socializing at family fiestas, weddings, and quinceañeras had played an important role in family life. He had once served in the military and later worked three part-time jobs to put himself through college. He had worked for twenty-five years in parks and recreation, organizing community programs for "at-risk" youth. And he had been good at delivering services and programs that they could relate to. After all, he knew firsthand what it was like to grow up in a community pervaded by an atmosphere of hopelessness. Drug use, prostitution, violence, and gang-related activity were aspects of daily life back then. Many of those he went to school with were now either dead or in prison. Much later in life, when he thought about how well he and his brother and sister turned out, he concluded that it was the sacrifices his mother and father made (and the grace of God) that allowed him to escape the chaos and personal distress that so often grip those living at the social and economic margins.

That evening, he and Abigail went through their usual routine: he cooked dinner while Abigail's care worker, Mary, showered her and got her ready. They usually tried to eat dinner together, which wasn't always possible on the nights Ruth returned home late from work. But tonight, here they were, sitting together as a family.

Abigail poked a finger into the pile of whipped potatoes on her plate and scooped a finger-full into her mouth.

"That won't work," he laughed. "Pizza and hotdogs are OK for fingers, but for potatoes we use a spoon."

He gently placed a spoon in her hand and guided it to her mouth. Then, very very slowly, by herself, she lifted a heaped spoonful to her mouth, her eyes fixed ahead in full concentration. Their eyes locked and she smiled with a sense of pride and accomplishment. He relished these moments, for the very skills we commonly take for granted Abigail had to acquire through patience and persistent practice; and though feeding her was still a time-consuming process, she was slowly learning to do it by herself. He was both proud of her achievements and in awe of the remarkable progress she'd made over the last six years.

He attributed much of Abigail's progress to the cessation of her seizures. Early on, their lives had been engulfed in human drama and complications. Abigail's life hung in the balance from the cataclysmic moment of Ruth's amniotic fluid leak at fifteen weeks. They had decided they were going to fight for her existence regardless of the consequences. Despite the fearful apprehension that accompanied their journey into parenthood, nothing could prepare them for the love and trepidation, familiar to most parents, that gripped them the moment she opened her lungs for the first time.

But Abigail's tumultuous journey had only just begun. She experienced a hemorrhage at birth and developed hydrocephalus as a result, which would later become the basis of her cerebral palsy diagnosis. By the time she was six she had already undergone over twenty neurosurgical operations because of shunt complications. Early on, it had been her fragile health status and seizures that prompted Raul to retire. Back then, Ruth was earning more money in her career and he was nearer retirement age anyway. They had decided that they could no longer in good conscience leave Abigail in the hands of paid caregivers, relative strangers, given her complex needs and their deep conviction that they would do a better job caring for her.

They had several paid caregiverss over the years, provided by the Arizona Department of Economic Security, which they were extremely grateful for. They knew, as do most families caring for dependents, that paid caregivers can be an essential piece of one's care network, enabling parents to meet expectations that are typically a self-evident ingredient of parenthood, like maintaining financial stability and a semblance of leisure time. But the sad truth was they had struggled to find someone who could carry out the intensive labor Abigail required with the kind of responsivity and emotional investment they believed was integral to meeting her care needs.

There was one exception. There had been a caregiver some time ago that they'd been fond of. She had displayed the degree of emotional engagement with Abigail that they yearned for in a paid caregiver. And Raul had loved watching them together: the way she danced with Abigail and sang to her. Then, late one afternoon, he'd returned home a little earlier from his errands than expected. Through the side window of the house he could see the caregiver asleep on the couch, barely visible underneath a blanket. Abigail was all alone in her room, sitting on the edge of her bed, vulnerable to falling. He was horrified. They had to let her go. Since then, no one had been able to fill her shoes.

That night, he was woken by Abigail squealing. The night-waking problems had started a year ago. He would inevitably give in and check on her, but not now; for now, he would resist, hoping that she would stop so that he could stay comfortably sprawled out in bed next to Ruth. By the fifth scream, though, he had climbed out of bed and was walking calmly down the wide hallway to her bedroom. Through the open door he could see her sitting in bed with her arms stretched out toward the crucifix hanging on the wall. He remembered, then, a priest once telling him that children with disabilities sometimes have a divine connection to God.

Most people who knew Abigail knew she was deeply religious; after all, Raul had passed his religiosity on to her. Despite her limited communicative capacities, she loved listening to prayers over her augmentative and alternative communication system while holding her rosary beads. But he found himself reticent to initiate those who didn't share their faith into her late-night communions with the supramundane. And, frankly, he loathed the thought of reliving these divine moments through the perceptions of others who might coopt and integrate them into their own interpretive line of secular reasoning. Better to keep what he witnessed close, he reasoned, where it could endure unscathed.

The next morning, he woke up earlier than usual. He drank a cup of coffee, ate a piece of dry toast, and finished the weekly spreadsheet detailing the family's budget. Then he returned to his bedroom where he finished getting dressed, before waking Abigail up and getting her off to school. Usually she caught the bus to school, which was only a few blocks away, because she enjoyed riding with the other kids. But today was the beginning of fall semester and so he decided to take her in himself. The weather was cooling, fall was beginning to lend its hues to the landscape, and snowbirds were plugging up roads and frustrating residents across the Valley of the Sun.

As part of the school breakfast program at Abigail's elementary school, students attending special education classes joined the general population in the cafeteria for breakfast, instead of eating the meal alone in their classrooms. In fact, Raul and Ruth had been at the forefront of the initiative. That morning, though, he was displeased to find Abigail's classmates eating breakfast in the classroom, away from the rest of the school kids. When he questioned the classroom aid about it, she insisted the cafeteria staff were at fault: "They said the kids take too long to eat."

He felt angry as well as sorry for the kids, and his indignation carried him off to Principal Todd's office. He was told that Todd was busy and soon found himself crossing paths with Naomi, the school's speech pathologist. She was in her late twenties and he liked her. She was good at her job and was always kind to him. Naomi invited him back to her office, and he was grateful for the chance to vent his frustrations.

"What?!" she responded when he told her what he'd seen.

"Is that insensitive or what?"

"What?!" she repeated, her face seized by incredulity.

Although he was still deflated, he felt a gust of comfort from her vindication of his outrage. "So just be aware that that's going on over there," he added. "If you can talk to the cafeteria staff and see what you can do—"

"Yeah. I'll do that today, for sure," she said.

He was about to leave when she said, with a kind of admiration he found thrilling, "By the way, I just heard about the resource fair."

"Well my wife did this—"

"Which is totally awesome," she said.

Like most parents, in the beginning Raul and Ruth knew very little about their world of disability. And like most parents, they lacked the practical skills needed to find their way around the medical bureaucracies and social spaces in which people in their situation become immersed. Even though they were both college-educated, learning the language of doctors and insurance companies had proven demanding. It was during this time that they became acutely aware of the inequities affecting Hispanic families caring for disabled children within their community. Many of these children were living in low-income, Spanish language-only households. The language barrier was affecting the use of services by these families.

The more Raul adjusted to his world of disability, the more he found his thoughts turning toward issues of diversity and inclusion; toward the circumstances of parents and families affected by linguistic barriers, their limited awareness of available resources, their fears regarding stigma, and the financial constraints that deprived them of the opportunity to stay home and care for their disabled dependents. Through these concerns he discovered a renewed appreciation for the time he had been given with Abigail. Over the coming years he and Ruth drew on their shared propensity for community involvement (which had been such a big part of their former lives) and began focusing their time and energy on local projects that fostered inclusion and integration in the school and the community. The Latino Disability Resource Fair was their latest venture. It had been Ruth's brainchild, but he had climbed aboard proudly. It went some way, they believed, toward helping families access timely and appropriate resources that make life as a caregiver easier and that, ultimately, shape the potential life of the child.

"OK. OK. Well, she got money for it, the whole works, all the sponsors," he said. He could hear the prideful burst of enthusiasm in his voice, in his frenetic pacing. "She went to Todd, I was incensed, she says, 'OK Todd, I've done everything I can do. Can you please mail the flyers out to parents?' And he says no! How can you have a parent take all this time and energy and resources and not mail, I mean, what's the thing with mailing?"

"I'm not sure."

"So, if I have to, I will find out where the special needs classrooms are in every school and I'll give them out myself."

They talked a little longer. She asked him to keep her informed and he promised he would. And then he found himself walking out the door, leaving the school, and heading to Subway for lunch.

He took Abigail to the movies that evening. Afterward, they strolled around Walmart and watched the world around them. Abigail shared his natural sociability. If she spotted someone heading in her direction, she stretched her arm out of her wheelchair to greet them. Early on, Raul had been devastated to find people both unintentionally and deliberately ignoring her, averting their gaze or brushing past her indifferently. Once, she was so very deliberately ignored that she burst into tears. That episode had really worn away at him inside. It was his duty to protect her self-esteem. It was then that he decided to anticipate her social overtures and inform her potential interlocutors of her intentions. "She wants to say hi to you," was his refrain. He found that most people, once he had explained the situation in this manner, responded favorably to her openness, either shaking her hand or sitting beside her and initiating a more intimate interaction. But there were always those who employed ruses to evade an encounter (a faux cell phone call was a classic), or those who remained standoffish and awkward, who couldn't seem to transcend whatever implicit behavioral contract Abigail undermined with her embodied differences. You could see in their painful tentativeness that they were afraid of saying the wrong thing. And once the awkwardness was in play there was no escaping it. It was like a vortex that pulled everyone in proximity down into its logically fallacious depths.

That night, as he tucked a sheet around Abigail, his body remembered what it had been like to hold her as a baby. It had been over twelve years since her birth and he rarely thought anymore about the obstacle course of dangers that characterized those early years. But he had never, not once, resented the exigencies of his situation. From the time he held her in the palm of his hand when she was just twenty-five weeks old and weighed one pound, he could feel something ineffable and gracious through her. She was tiny and fragile but stretched from the earth to the heavens. And it was his job, he told himself, to keep watch over her, to guard this earthly messenger and the secrets she carried.

EPISTEMIC COMMUNITIES AND THE EXISTENTIAL DEMANDS OF ETHICAL LIFE

Alignments between parents of disabled children cannot be taken for granted just because of an abstract notion concerning the loss of a shared dream or idealized child. Beyond an appreciation for the ways parents reinhabit the space of possibilities in which they contingently reside, the experiential category of "special needs parent" (or any other compound term that relegates parents to a particular class of disability) may not be that informative in terms of shared experience and footing. For many parents, the shared oppression of social exclusion matters more than their child's diagnosis.

The stress and coping literature often privileges the negative ways parents are impacted by their child's disability in order to more effectively convey the negative impacts on parents to those involved in health/education practices and service delivery.[14] In these accounts, the caregiving burden is treated as a pathological condition that needs to be overcome or rehabilitated. These approaches come at the expense of capturing the ways care is embodied by parents in relation to the particularities of their given existential situations and the bodies they care for. By contrast, I view caregiver burden and the moral modes of being that arise from it as foundational to subjectivity and ethical life.

While the labor involved in caring for disabled children comes with its own continuing personal, physical, and emotional challenges, "familiarity and routine," as author Helen Featherstone puts it, "blunt our awareness of disability after a while. Without meaning to, a stranger can upset this internal balance."[15] Even hard-won changes in familiarity can be precarious and quickly undermined through experiences of cultural marginalization, social isolation, and stigma.

Takoda's continued social alienation and misrecognition by others, that is, his frequent relegation to the outskirts of social and moral belonging, are inseparable from the emotional pain, exhaustion, and vulnerability to suffering that mark my experiences as his caregiver. These demands and difficulties are central to the ways care is embodied. Before he started school, a well-intentioned nurse remarked on the great strides we as a society have made in accepting and recognizing disability. She lent this notion support through a personal anecdote concerning a disabled child her children attend school with. She affirmed, "They pay no attention to his disability." She was kind in attempting to assuage whatever anxieties I had about Takoda starting school for the first time. But I found her allusion to society's corporeal blindness misguided. In fact, her words resounded distinctly in my mind one morning at kindergarten, as I watched Takoda attempt to ingratiate himself with two classmates. As two boys chased each other, he followed them, crawling to catch up, smiling excitedly. When they finally came to a standstill, they barely acknowledged that he was sitting happily at their feet, his eyes fixed on them. The nurse's words have lived in my mind ever since, rushing out of the shadows on other occasions too: how to do justice to the dizzying spell of emotions that arise when your fellow café patrons move tables after sighting your physically disabled child? That was when I realized how comfortable privilege and these misguided fallacies are to wear.

The idea of corporeal blindness is as specious to me as the belief that we live in a post-racial society, in which the color of one's skin has no relevance or political meaning. As critical race theorist and legal scholar Patricia Williams writes, while color-blindness can be held as a legitimate hope for the future, "the very notion of blindness about color constitutes an ideological confusion at best, and denial at its very worst."[16] As she puts it, these claims to blindness can leave people of color "pulled between the clarity of their own experience and the often alienating terms in which they must seek social acceptance."[17] Like race, the othering of disabled bodies through social practices that position and produce them as abnormal and/ or inferior can take on subtle forms across a range of material and social practices. It is certainly more comfortable to escape the stigma of ableism or avoid the discomfort of diversity work that we are all responsible for by maintaining that adequate social recognition and comprehensibility of those with disabilities has already been won. But I find this claim stands in stark opposition to the experiences of social discomfort and exclusion I share with other parents.[18]

Ethan put it this way: "It's that look on their [distant friends'/strangers'] face, that deer in the headlights look: 'Oh my God, you've confronted me with something that makes me horribly uncomfortable. I don't want to have to face this, it's too horrifying. I have kids of my own. I can't fathom what it would be like. Let me go back to my normal life, please.' And I get it. I do. It's human nature. It probably happens to everyone who has something that is vastly different. So often we isolate ourselves, so we don't have to see that look on their face. I'm not shocked as to why special needs parents get so angry and feel so slighted by society. If we feel that way, so marginalized. I know somewhere deep down inside Jack feels it. He's gotta. He's a human being. He has feelings. So if I'm feeling it, he's feeling it. It sucks. So it makes me mad. It makes me sad."

It is not only through these vicarious experiences of a child's stigmatization that parents face exclusion but also through the ways disability and family life are marginalized in a variety of cultural productions, for example, the media, literature, and film. While I was in the United States for my fieldwork in 2015, for example, an online initiative called *Sesame Street and Autism: See Amazing in All Children* was launched. The program was viewed by Sesame Workshop as a promising web-based platform offering educational videos about autism and resources for individuals on the spectrum and their families.[19] Julia, a Muppet with autism, was introduced as part of the initiative to help spread awareness and reduce stigma around autism.

The initiative was met with mixed feelings among the parents I spent time with on fieldwork. While some thought it would jump-start a cultural conversation around autism, others met the initiative with apprehension and concern. Ethan found it disquieting that Julia was relegated to the online program, rather than being a part of the mainstream show— once again, it seemed as though disability was being relegated to the cultural peripheries.[20] Other parents expressed concern over the ways autism would be represented. Would this social platform, for instance, represent those embodying more complex and challenging behaviors and what it takes for their families to survive, or would they be overshadowed by an agenda for inclusion based on autonomy and independence? Indeed, the disability rights agenda is often reluctant to admit to vulnerability and the divisions born of profound difference within its own cause. Jeanette Betancourt, Sesame Workshop's vice president of outreach and educational practices, certainly seemed to suggest as much when she proposed that, in order to breakdown misconceptions around autism, the producers "wanted to demonstrate some of the characteristics of autism in a positive way."[21]

While it's hard to imagine that anyone would disagree that sensitivity is a good thing, too much caution can potentially miss an important segment of the population affected by autism. That is to say, the tendency of the media and members of the neurodiversity movement to create apparent cohesion within the category of autism by representing only a portion of the spectrum—for instance, those with cognitive strengths and talents—can alienate members of the community whose experiences and needs are vastly different. One mother responded to the unnecessary cultural marginalization and social isolation of those raising profoundly disabled children by drawing attention to the sense of alienation that arises from only ever seeing disability framed by the media in regard to overcoming formidable odds: "Now, show me a picture of a kid in an involved wheelchair, with a vent, a g-tube pump and a suction device. Show me a kid with combined severe cognitive and physical disabilities. Talk about dystonia, spasm, tone, seizures, scoliosis, drop foot, silent aspiration. Show me the parent(s). Show me how they are living. In short...show me something that I can identify with. Show me something that acknowledges the existence of this type of disability and everything it entails. Openly discuss struggles as well as joys. Tell me, tell my kid that what is important is just getting on with our day to day lives as best we can, even without a specific contribution or goal or happy-ending-in-sight. We can be 'happy' and 'successful' if you broaden the definition of those words."

Emphasizing the effects these representational choices have on caregivers, essayist Scot Sea laments in a piece for the news and opinion website *Salon*: "New Age pests, overdosed on media mythology, overhear you are the parent of an autistic child and, eyes aglow, pronounce, 'Oh! And isn't that just a blessing?' In Wisconsin, storefront fundamentalists suffocate an 8-year-old autistic boy to death while attempting to 'exorcise' his strange behaviors....Clueless neighbors, whose own children run wild, devoid of discipline, remark, 'Yeah, our kids are just like her—'cept we got three of them.'"[22]

Admitting to the existence of disorder and the burden of caregiving is not without its ethical quandaries. After all, it can legitimate dehumanizing views of disability, especially in a society where negative connotations associated with disability abound. Scot said he was vilified by some readers for the *Salon* piece. Those who have read the essay might perceive him as an activist who speaks to what philosopher Ian Hacking refers to as "the family-shattering impact of severe autism."[23] I present a passage from Scot's essay because his narrative captures the anaerobic conditions of fatigue and endurance that can sometimes permeate parents' experiences of caregiving. He writes:

The deeper into brutal night she marathons the more wired, delirious, hyper-manic she becomes. Daylight seems to click her down a few amps. She seems alert and ready for the day. A full circle has transpired and now, a familiar morning ritual. Calming, predictable. Breakfast. More pills. Hair. Teeth. Dressed. (Help your 15-year-old daughter on with her bra every morning and the female breast loses most of its mystery.) Get her on the bus. Now you must leave for work. Can't take any more sick days. So sleepwalk through the motions. Hope your reserves kick in. Take an early lunch. Doze in the car for an hour. Throw down three cups of mud stewing since morning. Limp 'til 5:30. Collapse at home. Sleep through midnight. Again, your wife wakes you. Yeah, she's still up, she informs you—napped two hours at school, cruising ever since. Your wife has clients tomorrow. She must crash. Time for your shift.[24]

I met Scot and his wife, Patty, in 2015 after reading his autobiographical essay on autism for *Salon*. The piece had been published twelve years earlier, when their daughter, Jessie, was sixteen. At that time of our meeting she had been dead for a little over a year. Her early exit from the world at the age of twenty-seven from kidney disease had left an irrevocable absence in their lives that was very much present during our time together (glimpsed in all manner of gestures and looks between them). The space they would have to remake for themselves was still very much under construction. Scot said, "She could just never catch a break. It was this and that. She couldn't communicate, she was thoroughly intellectually delayed, she had seizures, as well as GI issues, and she gets polycystic kidneys from me."

That afternoon, in the warm shade on the back patio of their home, I asked Scot why he wrote the piece. "I can tell you exactly my reason," he said unflinchingly. "I'd finally had it with seeing these—you'd see them in like lifestyle magazines or Sunday paper supplements and they always had the same title: how my diabetic cousin inspires me or how my niece with cerebral palsy taught me bravery. Or they're authored by some television celebrity or some athlete's wife, you know? And the photo is always of— they're all well-clothed, in a big grassy backyard with a golden retriever, a twenty-four-hour nanny, and a six-figure salary, and everything is fine. Things don't look that bad. And I remember reading these things and saying to myself, you want to know what it's like?"

There was silence. And then he added drily, "So that's why I wrote the piece."

Hacking notes that autism narratives not only describe one's reality but also help forge the concepts in which to think about this unstable category.[25] With so much at stake, there are sometimes heated exchanges between parents and families of severely disabled children and members of the neurodiversity movement. The positive celebration of autism as cognitive difference, that link with broader sociopolitical themes concerning representation, identity, and the ultimate position of those with disabilities and autism in society, is a source of tension between them.[26] These heated public exchanges are often carried out over social media platforms, but they are not necessarily limited to autism. It's important to recognize that uncomfortable tensions can arise anywhere different types of knowledge and experience exist. According to the Seas, there was a clear bipolarity in the feedback Scot received for his *Salon* article, between those commending his bravery in giving a voice to the visceral character of the daily lives of families caring for autistic individuals and those condemning his account as offensive and fearmongering.

In his book, *NeuroTribes*, Steve Silberman mentions how terrifying Scot's piece is for families grappling with a child's diagnosis and seeking information on the internet.[27] Arguably, the most contentious aspect of Scot's essay, and the part that Silberman takes to task, is the way he extends his sympathy to Delfin Bartolome, a fifty-five-year-old father of three, who murdered his twenty-seven-year-old autistic son in 2002 before turning the gun on himself. By all accounts, Delfin was a devoted husband and father.[28] His nephew is reported saying that he never had the impression that Delfin saw his son as an immense burden, or that he felt unduly weighed down caring for his family.[29] Speculating about Delfin's motives for the murder-suicide, Silberman writes, he "had been laid off just before retirement, shunting him into a series of temporary jobs and putting his son's future care at risk."[30]

It is fairly obvious why anyone would be outraged by someone who would kill their disabled child, even if it's also evident how much pressure they were under at the time. So why did Scot feel the need to extend the empathetic imagination to Delfin's viewpoint? By drawing attention to Delfin's case, Scot aims to draw attention not only to the pressures of caregiving but also to the impact of living in a society where the most vulnerable and their families are frequently mistreated. In Scot's view, if families are to approximate a normal quality of life, then respite and community support and services are essential. In short, the Delfin tragedy reveals a world where autonomy is limited by the acknowledgement of our profound dependency.

"There are legislators here whose grandchildren were autistic, had no idea what that was during their careers in politics," Scot told me, sitting back in his chair as he spoke. "They probably didn't have much patience from constituents who were telling them about these obscure lifestyle wars they were waging until it happened to them."

Scot feels that representing the suffering and vulnerability of caregivers is necessary in order to get the attention of legislators who have the power to change public policy and therefore help guard families against the inexplicable vulnerabilities that arise in desperate situations. In a quest to emphasize the importance of community support and respite services for families, Scot wrote the *Salon* piece to forcibly demonstrate what it takes to endure the exhaustion and monotony of caring for one's remarkable and impossible child and what it looks like "to make a life on a different planet," where, as he puts it, "the gravity is strong. And the climate rarely changes."[31]

He told me that an issue that continues to vex him is industry's indifference to employees who are "swallowed up in impossible family logistics." He said, "There are only so many times managers are willing to be patient while an IT staffer must flee the office because their kid is seizuring again. Of course, if they were stranded because of a flight cancellation there would be no questions asked. Who's to say that same IT gal doesn't have the potential of developing a million-dollar app for that company? The blood researcher whose intellectual attention is halved fifty percent because home aids keep quitting. What if they are on the verge of curing diabetes? CEOs must recognize that it is *in their interest*, their bottom line's interest to accommodate these anonymous workers. Progressive human resources departments should create, I dunno, offices of special needs within their bodies. At least in my utopia."

The story of the plight of disabled individuals and the families caring for them—their unjustifiable marginalization from mainstream society and institutional discrimination—is well known, and yet it can be glimpsed everywhere. For instance, in 2015, the *New York Times* reported a story about a United Airlines flight that was redirected from Portland to Salt Lake City for an emergency landing after the crew decided an autistic child's disruptive behavior warranted removing the family from the aircraft.[32] The incident began, according to the article, after Ms. Beegle requested to purchase a hot meal for her daughter, Juliette, in order to keep her settled. The flight attendant, for whatever reason, refused, offering her a sandwich instead. Juliette had a meltdown and was eventually accommodated with a hot meal to settle her. But by then, an emergency landing was already underway. Whatever the circumstances of the family's removal were, negative attitudes toward disability are voiced in the comments section after the article. The comments can be easily divided into two camps (the most hostile comments aside): those sympathetic toward the plight of Ms. Beegle and her daughter and those displaying the kind of ignorance and misunderstanding that support the social estrangement experienced by families and the cultural disavowal of their children:

"If... her daughter required a hot meal, why didn't she book first class tickets."

"Rules still apply to them."

"Other people have their own problems."

"If you know your autistic child will... act out... Stay home or drive places."

"Stay home and lock your kid in a closet seems to be what you're recommending," one parent responded. "That was fashionable in the 19th century and early 20th centuries. Sorry, I'm just not down with that solution. Thankfully things have changed a little. But obviously not enough."

This brings us back to the issue of representation. As Hamington and Rosenow point out, "Information is an essential prerequisite of care because it is difficult, if not impossible, to care for someone or something that is entirely unknown."[33] As Scot alluded to in his justification for writing the *Salon* piece, some parents caring for children with autism, many of whom also have an intellectual disability and other learning difficulties and are unable to speak for themselves, feel like they are being culturally overlooked and marginalized. Not recognizing the heterogeneity within autism itself is a problem. It poses risks to research that could help those suffering from autism's most severe challenges. It also risks marginalizing the intimate experiences of families caring for autistic individuals who will struggle with particular challenges their entire lives.

The uncomfortable tensions between parents caring for children who require advocacy on their behalf and those with disabilities who have the ability to effectively advocate for themselves often play out on social media platforms, such as Twitter. For example, in an exchange oriented around the politics of representation, a Twitter user, responding to a post written by disability rights activist Gregg Beratan, conveyed her dismay over parents' refusal to "accept/love their kids," criticizing them for thinking that "their experience trumps all." Gregg responded, "And that's my big issue with awareness campaigns never moves onto acceptance they don't even shed the idea that we are broken."[34] But for parents caught in the monotony, stress, and exhaustion of intimate caregiving and dealing with the maladaptive behaviors and other co-occurring conditions that overlap with autism, pathologizing a child's disability might not seem like a stretch, nor a question of love.

Some self-advocates claim that they are in a better position than others to understand those who are nonverbal and interminably dependent. Some parents, however, see a distance too immutable between the children they care for and the embodied situation of self-advocates for their insights to be of any practical import. As Ethan said, "I'm a human. He's a human. Humanity is a large spectrum. Doesn't mean one end knows jack dick about the other." These tensions touch on an important issue regarding who is morally qualified to speak on behalf of whom—an issue that has troubled my own academic discipline of anthropology.[35]

Some parents might find accounts like Scot's offensive on the premise that his representation rhetorically dehumanizes those with autism or other disabilities by publicly representing them as sources of misery and hardship. Others may suggest that such accounts reek of self-pity. But with such large swathes of public ignorance on display, like the comments underneath the airline article that show a lack of genuine care for others, just what kind of disclosures should be made? For an example, let me return to Scot's essay for a moment. A sibling of an autistic man responded in the comments section that his brother is gainfully employed and has an active social life thanks to the loving support of his family and the strong educational background they provided him with. "I don't 'feel' for the man who killed his child and himself," he writes. "Did he exhaust every opportunity for his child's development?" The comment reflects commonly held moral values about what makes our lives human and how we should conduct them, for example, culturally celebrated notions of purposive agency and achievement. Many parents, however, might challenge these norms. For them, seeking to live a good life in terms of self-determination and choice is not an option.

Conflicting interests and definitions of the good make the moral arena fraught with ambiguity and disagreement. As Hatab writes, "We sometimes fail in our aim for the good, or in doing good we sometimes instigate harmful effects.... Ethical commitments often require risk and sacrifice, which makes anxiety and mixed dispositions inevitable."[36] While some stories have the potential to instigate harmful effects by playing into the long-standing equation of disability with tragedy, undermining the strides the disability community has made in trying to break with demeaning stereotypes and create a sense of identity around disability, others stories can combat public ignorance by adding to the social fund of knowledge about disability, with the hope of engendering social tolerance and acceptance.

I disagree with some people's claims that Scot's account amounts to hateful rhetoric. My conversations with Scot and Patty made it clear that Scot loved his daughter deeply. From the perspective of parents, the moral calculus is complicated. Caregiving entails the irreducible confluence of exhaustion and love. To sympathize with the situation in which murder-suicides such as the one Scot describes arise is not to endorse them. For example, Paul admits to hoping for the "mother ship" to come for Pearl or for a tear in the fabric of space-time to swallow them both up. "I'm into this twenty-three years," he says. "I'm fifty-six and I have to worry about whether Pearl will outlive me." The numbing monotony of caregiving and the social isolation and exhaustion that permeate caregivers' experiences can lead to internal inconsistencies, and sometimes human and moral tragedy.

The neurodiversity movement correctly draws our attention to the neurodiverse nature of our minds. It has done so by highlighting the neurological variation intrinsic to our identities. Nonetheless, it is vital to recognize the importance of freedom of expression in the public discourse on autism and disability and the importance of shared stories and the solidarity they can engender. The argument for inclusion has often come at the expense of those without the ability to speak up for themselves. The parents and families that care for those individuals could benefit from making their difficult situations more culturally visible. We need to consider the breadth of diversity within diagnostic classifications and appraise accounts ethically through the lens of justice, that is, if we think of justice as learning to tolerate difference and ambiguity.

AN UNCERTAIN INHERITANCE

We drive down a gray ribbon of highway that stretches across the desert and then falls away into the distance. We're heading back to Phoenix after a weekend in Las Vegas with family. It's a four-and-a-half-hour trip back to Scottsdale, but we are taking our time, enjoying the desert's vast and magnificent solitude. Two hours in, we stop at an In-N-Out to get lunch and refuel. From the register I can see Takoda in the back seat of our car, staring out the window, his little mouth hanging slightly open.

A door in my mind is opened. "Suzie calls them window lickers when she sees them on a bus," my father said, sometime not too long ago. "Me though, I just feel sorry for them," he had added, in his typical self-aggrandizing manner.

I wrongly thought that I had grown immune to his barbs over our previous years of estrangement. His verbal onslaught left me feeling hurt and indignant. At that time, he hadn't met Takoda yet. And the more I thought about it, the more I loathed the thought of them meeting. I simply didn't have the emotional agility or wherewithal to vicariously experience whatever discomfiting feelings my son would awaken in him. Why? Because I have spent a great deal of energy reckoning with familial projections and social attitudes around disability, which began to claw at the walls of my consciousness a long time ago. It hasn't been easy. These projections and attitudes can keep the most well-meaning of us ensconced in ignorance, limiting our selfhood in indefinable ways. It's not only a child's disability and the social experience it brings that add to parental ambivalence. I suspect many parents reckon with the tyranny of internalized prejudices and the deep aching of sorrow that can become such a constant part of their experience.

This is my life.

Admittedly, at times I feel like I'm living someone else's.

Hopeless.

"I hope you don't feel like you have this bleak future," Ethan said to me before I left the Midwest.

Unmet expectations had in fact been a deep source of disappointment and confusion. I confessed I was trying to surrender to the present, expectation-free, which was becoming harder to do.

"You have to have some level of hopeful, positive energy," he added. "Not that he'll get up and walk and talk and dance and do those things, but the answers will open up."

After a long pause, he continued, "It's not for me to say. I'm in a totally different situation. So, I don't know."

And then: "I feel bad for you."

"Don't feel bad for me," I snapped back, irritated.

"It's not pity."

"I know."

"It's not that."

His exhortation felt empty, like a mask he was putting on for my benefit. From what I had seen, Ethan was dwelling in contradiction, trapped in the dark recesses of his memories, locked in corrosive grief. If love and care can mold an identity, so can exhaustion and despair.

We plunge back onto Highway 93, fringed by low mountains. Sun on my face. Soothed by the flow of cold air from the air conditioning.

"No expectations without experience," the historian Reinhart Koselleck writes, "no experience without expectation."[37] I felt like there was something absent from my experience. The radical contingency that governs human life had stolen the power of expectation from me and the intelligible world it fosters. What form could any substantial hope take in the face of such uncertainty? If hope is the confluence of desire and confidence, or an investment in an assumption, as philosopher and political theorist Philip Pettit suggests, that galvanizes thought and action, it felt out of my reach.[38] Desire and confidence seemed worlds apart.

I was following a road unknown to myself. I had wandered from the designated path and all the types of idiosyncratic and cultural meanings that defined its contours: the individual and collective activities, anticipations, aspirations, and potential future life events that comprise our meaningful possibilities. I felt suspended in the presence of the unknown. Writing about the uncertainty of human existence in the face of what lies beyond our control, composer and philosopher Leonard Meyer notes, "We anxiously await the breaking of the storm, the discovery of what unrelenting fate has decreed."[39] This general state of suspense, he says, involves a set of nonspecific expectations that make us sensitive to a range of possibilities grounded in past experience, beliefs, and attitudes.[40] What kind of hope could I hope to inhabit in this state of suspension, when the horizon of expectation that gives a sense of familiarity to our indefinite possibilities had abandoned me?

Ethan seemed so sensitive to every tremor and evidence of failure that I wasn't sure how useful his brand of hope was. Although I had initially been interested in how participation in Earl's support groups could help men (including me) reframe their experiences of disability and facilitate meaningful social connections, I found his Leibniz-esque doctrine of divine providence unsatisfying: that God is perfect and so, then, are all existing things in the universe. "Every child is uniquely designed," he preached, and "each parent is distinctly right for their child." In fact, competing definitions over the purpose of the support group I attended seemed to be a source of dissonance among some attendees and perhaps explained its premature plateau in numbers. In the beginning, my attendance seemed to heighten participants' awareness of and interactions with each other, which was cause for all kinds of emotionally charged discussions during these sparsely populated meetings.

At one meeting, Brent, a father of a prepubescent boy with disabilities, remarked that his friend has kids with serious drug problems who have been incarcerated. "He has a hard time believing your philosophy that we are the right fathers for our kids and that they're the right kids for us," he said. "He feels like there's no way he could be the right father to his kids with the lives they've had."

Earl's face visibly fell in on itself as he lowered it from Brent's gaze, nodding tolerantly. "But the alternative that we're not is pretty bleak," he said. "What quality of life would that bring?"

At least to me, rational instrumentality seems beyond the province of belief. As sensible as Pascal's wager may be, it seems outside the realm of discretionary control.

For others, hope seemed too compatible with self-deception. At least that's the way it appeared to me then. Doug retold the same story over and over again with an inseparable mix of anguish and joy: Noah, his eldest, was graduating from middle school, so he took him suit shopping so he would have something nice to wear for the ceremony. "It was a solid looking Johnny Cash outfit," he told me, "and we found this burgundy fedora-style hat and bow tie to match. He came to the full-length mirror outside the changerooms and just stopped and stood real tall and said, *you know, I'm starting to feel like a young man.* It just blew my mind," Doug recalled, tears sitting stagnant in the bottom of his eyes. "He is so far ahead of what we expected," he continued. "Not that we didn't hope that he would be here, but just from where he was six years ago, even two years ago, that's not the young man that I would have expected to see at this point. But he's killing it, socially and academically. He's really smart. They're *both* really smart, you know."

In light of Nick's severe behavioral problems, I felt like Doug's coming of age tale about Noah circled more around *Nick's* potentiality. That is, the hope that he would one day reach a similar point in his development and being, despite all evidence pointing to the contrary.

And how was I supposed to make sense of the profound contradictions between Paul's experiences of caregiving for Pearl and the ways he narratively communicated them at various times? This discernible gap seemed to speak to a hope that was shot through and through with the beclouding effects of self-deception. Paul often talked about having hope for an easier future. He seemed to recognize beyond all doubt the oppressive cultural beliefs and social practices that make caregiving and life for those with disabilities difficult—after all, most of his blogs were geared toward describing these experiences—and yet, at times, he managed to hide these perturbations from himself.

For example, anthropologist and prolific blogger William Peace made a point of criticizing the transportation industry and continued use of school segregation for perpetuating negative perceptions around disability. He writes: "Are we unable to incorporate and educate those that think differently and not at the typical, perhaps demanded, pace? The answer to all these questions is yes. By itself this is damning to our educational system and the culture that created and perpetuates it."[41]

Peace's blog elicited a particularly defensive reaction from Paul, who responded to the piece with a blog of his own, denouncing Peace's claims that the accessible bus is sometimes referred to by other school kids as the "retard bus"—suggesting that Peace, who has been paralyzed since he was eighteen years old, was projecting these negative perceptions about disability onto others. Paul emphatically stated that Pearl has not experienced any social alienation, discrimination, or battle for accommodation, and that any discrimination they have faced has come from the pervasive social norm that men shouldn't be involved in the intimate care of young women. After everything he'd already disclosed to me, I couldn't help but wonder if his embrace of hope for an easier future somehow required an illusion about the way things were.

That night, after parting ways with Ethan, in the frigid darkness of my hotel room on the outskirts of Columbus, I cried: my body seismic and despondent, hot tears running down my face. I remembered Paul's words from sometime earlier, from a blog post that curled its way into a corner of my memory long ago: "It hits you out of nowhere. You think everything will be OK, at this point you can handle anything. Bullshit. Like an unexpected left hook, life just crashes. . . . I will never die having seen my child get a diploma. Lots of people die in that situation. It was not my plan. Not my hope. Not my dream. I will never walk my daughter down the aisle. Never be proud of her accomplishments. And no, it's not about not loving what I have, what they are, and if you think that's what it is about, well fuck you too."

Facing the uncertainties of Takoda's life and health and what caring for him would look like had opened a chasm I would have to live with, but I didn't yet know how to. Regardless of the progression of time and no matter how much I learned over the coming years, I felt like there would always be this deep abyssal unfamiliarity and fear of not being good enough to face the changes and challenges he would need me to confront.

I usually feel at home in the desert. I love the buzz of my body under the burning desert sky and the intensely pleasurable feeling of aliveness that the breathless hot air awakens in me. Succulents grow abundantly out here, bold and distinct against the dry and inhospitable landscape. But driving back to Scottsdale—my son quietly sitting in the back seat—I feel a great distance between myself and the uncompromising life and beauty of the desert. My fieldwork had been full of carbon copy and contrast, contradiction and inconsistency. I needed time to sort out the alienation and discontent that had become integral to my craggy emotional landscape.

Anxieties surrounding fatherhood and my research engulf me. Thoughts of inadequacy, on both fronts, wake me during the night's deepest hours. Fieldwork, the hallmark of anthropology, has been more challenging than I anticipated. Often, it's carried out in places that aren't familiar to the anthropologist. Often, this is the point. For me, however, this couldn't have been further from the case, both geographically and in subject matter. My life as a father to a son with profound disabilities and my research into the lives of parents affected by disability in America are intimately connected. They are irreducible. There is no respite from my research topic. My intimate world of disability always awaits me.

We're approaching Phoenix's city limits. The megalopolis begins to surround us, stretching across the desert landscape, lapping at saguaro-peppered mountains. One desert slowly bleeds into another, the natural one into the suburban sprawl. For now, I am more at home in the nature-defying sunbelt city, amid the noise, neon signs, and franchise restaurants.

COMMUNITIES OF CARE AND CORPOREAL DIVERSITY

Eighteen months later, we pull off Italian motorway 93 into a gas station in the foothills of the Alps to buy a motorway vignette to cross over into Austria.

We have planned some recovery time in Lake Garda in northeast Italy before flying back to Melbourne. We have spent the last two weeks in the spa town of Bad Aibling in Germany. Despite its suspiciously ostentatious sound, I have been cooped up in a hospital room with my wife and two daughters for the last two weeks. Having spent the better half of the year bedridden, conventional regimens failing, symptoms raging unabated, we decided I should come to Bad Aibling's St. George Hospital for whole-body hyperthermia treatment. By then, I had been in a progressive state of decline, my physical and mental health, and the identities attached to them, steadily deteriorating. If there was a chance that the supposed bor-relia spirochetes colonizing me would be rendered defenseless under the extreme heat of hyperthermia (107.2 °F), then I was happy to be basted and cooked.

The rugged, snow-dusted Kaiser mountains bear down on me from around the gas station. The treatment has taken a toll on my body and I still feel weak with nausea and fatigue. The cold air runs its icy fingers along my skin. I gently close my eyes.

This is my life. Life is happening.

I have lost time. I have lost the first twelve months of my youngest daughter's life.

When I open them, I'm looking at the cloud-covered mountains. Everything up there is calm and still.

Inside the gas station restaurant, there is a young man sitting next to a boy in a wheelchair. The boy's mouth is open, and his eyes are fixed skyward. The man is eating, one hand resting on the boy's arm. At first, I think they are father and son but on closer inspection they look like broth-ers. Kim is standing next to me. She gently places a hand on the small of my back and I can tell she is feeling the way I do: we miss Takoda.

I remember Paul saying, "That is the dichotomy: given the chance to put Pearl in a residential facility and spend the last third of my life doing the things I desire, I choose not to."

We had hemmed and hawed about taking Takoda on my doctoral field-work. But in the end, despite the logistical burdens of travel, we decided it was important for him to be with us, for us to be united as a family. After all, our nonverbal interworld was the inspiration for my research. But this time, in my great illness, it was too difficult a task to bring him along, both logistically and emotionally.

We buy terrible-tasting coffee and head back to the car. I close my eyes and strain to occupy that same space as before, the chill on my skin, to feel that same cosmic whisper, but now there is nothing.

Illness stripped me of an enticing future, compounding the loss of per-sonal meanings Takoda's disability confronted me with. There was a point in my illness when time flattened out before me and I lost the capacity to hope for anything at all. Slowly, with the love of my family and Kim's enduring care, I managed to pull myself from the tormenting abyss of hopelessness, forever touched by the humility of being cared for. On the fringes of that existential dead zone I realized something important: the capacity to hope is different from not having any hope at all.

Takoda's disability catalyzed the decay of some of my purposes and hopes, which exacerbated my feelings of estrangement from others. In the face of such uncertainties, I was curious about how parents find new significances in their lives, how they forge a meaningful life and future in the face of life's uncompromising blend of freedom and necessity. Specifically, I wondered how my participants retained hope, as they claimed they did, when they testified to having all their hopes vanquished.

I had been wrong! I knew that now. It wasn't that their hopes were shot through and through with illusion or self-deception. It was much simpler than that. It was a choice to invest in more encouraging prospects and not get swept up in the unstable tides of experience and evidence. Sure, caregiving can entail lost possibilities, limitations to what the future may look like or hold. But the parents I spent time with hadn't lost the space of possibilities that make new possibilities seem imaginable.[42] Rather, caregiving had induced what philosopher Matthew Ratcliffe describes as "a modification of the 'style' in which one hopes."[43] The grounds of their taken-for-granted intentional hopes may have eroded, but they still had hope. They inhabited an *existential hope*: a hope that the answers might open up or that things would get easier in time.

There was a Camusian logic to achieving a sense of familiarity or control for parents that, paradoxically, involved acknowledging the world's ephemeral and elusive character, its "unreasonable silence."[44] Accepting one's fate freely involves an appreciation for immediacy, spontaneity, and pleasure, as well as a tempestuous adherence to finding meaning in what one has, for what other choice is there?

Pondering his future, Earl said thoughtfully, "I don't think we'll ever retire because of our life and who we are and what we've been through. We'll continue to move forward, and I want to support and encourage people to accept what life has given them and enjoy it." Paul also admitted to investing his confidence in the small and tangible things that make life worthwhile in the face of life's painful vicissitudes. "I stopped asking God why a long time ago. I'm more or less a day-to-day kind of guy," he said. Another time he said: "I could put Pearl in residential living logistically.

Not emotionally. There's thoughts toward maybe buying the house next door and turning it into a group home."

Ratcliffe refers to existential hope as a kind of "pre-intentional hope" that plays a distinctive phenomenological role.[45] It may be devoid of specific contents, but what remains is the possibility of new possibilities, "an orientation that is presupposed by the possibility of hoping."[46] Gradually, by retaking a stand on my existence against the threats wrought by illness, I experienced a return of hope or possibility in my life and came to understand this important distinction. By embracing one's life and unalterably changed circumstances, parents inhabit a hopefulness that anthropologist Angela Garcia says "presents a picture of the moral that embraces its own vulnerability and unpredictability."[47]

If the relationships we form are the essence of human meaning, then having a disabled child adds another dimension to that meaning. Changes in one's circumstances produces changes in one's subjective grasp on the world. The demands of care knock one out of their familiar world and impel a reconfiguration of one's habitual way of thinking, doing, knowing, and relating to the world. The everyday inconspicuousness that Martin Heidegger identifies as characteristic of our average being-with-one-another or mattering-to-one-another can thrust caregivers into mindful being-with-others.[48] Of course, parents are not equal to the demands of care, for each must remake a self in accordance with the new paths instituted by care and in relation to the referential contexts of their lives. Throughout this book I have been exploring the ways parents reinhabit these various horizons—temporal, cultural, social, spatial, intersubjective, gendered, imaginative, and ethical.

By associating with their own contingency and recognizing our profound dependency as human beings, parents often show a concern for the well-being of other caregivers and the selfhood of disabled children, speaking to what Arthur Frank calls a "communicative body," one that "sees reflections of its own suffering in the bodies of others," turning outward in "dyadic relatedness."[49] Earl, for instance, was committed to others through the support groups he ran in Arizona. And many other men had established online blogs to commune with others—those that did not participate in these online configurations of communication often expressed a desire to do so. Early on, Scot regularly attended local support meetings for parents. He said, "In the beginning it [testifying] was very satisfying. It was like a thirst or having a good meal. You're trading your stories and you're talking to families who have the same thing in common and enough of that goes by and it's like tools in your belt."

The online communities that parents of children with disabilities participate in are a salient medium for socially engaging and connecting with one's horizontal community. These emergent universes of storytelling and cultural convergence can be seen as cosmopolitan spaces, where individuals, sometimes from substantially different sociocultural, geographic, and intersectional backgrounds, come together through their shared experiences of caregiving, forming deep bonds of mutual understanding in the process. Through these online collaborative engagements, parents are given the opportunity to share their stories, exchange information, share grievances and struggles that those in one's local world may not understand, discuss experiences of alienation and exclusion (and other problems, both theoretical and pragmatic), alongside strategies and victories as they advocate for inclusion and equality. These shared online spaces are characterized by mutual collaboration, respect, and a concern for social justice. The particularities around caregiving that arise within local worlds intersect here with a global community of parents and bring forth caregiving practices rooted in an ethic of universal inclusion and moral respect for all persons. These online spaces of cultural convergence can be thought of as moral cosmopolitan communities.

These caregiving communities are strengthened through parents' emotional and ideological commitments to countering the hegemony of ableism, creating more accessible communities, and engendering a reality that validates and advances the rights and well-being of all kinds of embodiments. These communities facilitate storytelling, affording parents the opportunity to share with the public narratives that throw light on their child's capacity to ethically affect others. Paul said, "My kids taught me love unconditionally, how to appreciate the little and big things, that without perspective we have nothing." Similarly, now waxing pensively, Ethan wrote about seeing his son for who he is, a boy who loves to sing the ABC song by rote; not understanding it as an alphabet, Ethan said, but as a game that ends with daddy clapping and him jumping up and down, saturated with joy.

Parents' efforts speak to the humanitarian aspects of cosmopolitan activism, which are grounded in a shared recognition of our ineluctable but different forms of dependency, of the value of caregiving to society, of the fact that suffering is not necessarily inimical to life, and that there are ways of inhabiting the world and affecting others that depart from the mental qualities we usually associate with moral agency: in short, a recognition of human unity by virtue of our differences. One could argue that it is the act and experience of caregiving itself that turns caregivers into moral cosmopolitans. This emotional resonance with difference is the basis upon which caregivers come together and support one another. Caregiving narratives can offer radical hope to caregivers and, in their telling, demand of listeners an interest and concern for the life, existential vulnerability, and possibilities of others.

The stories caregivers share carry important social and political implications, because reading stories is one means by which we can nurture and develop our empathetic imaginations. Hamington and Rosenow present poetry as an aesthetic experience that can inspire moral change by providing an opportunity for the audience to cultivate the skills of openness and availability necessary for "meeting the unique strangeness of the other."[50] "When mapped on to real world human interactions," they write, these skills can "contribute to the ethical skill of caring."[51] While stories and poetry are different media and engender different affects and meanings, stories, like poetry, provide readers the opportunity to imaginatively try on new thoughts and feelings and transcend their identities and find alternate grounds for identification with those outside their sphere of experience.

While the personal resonance we find in stories and our possibilities for imaginatively inhabiting them reflect the lifeworlds we inhabit, they require us to project ourselves into realities different from our own. Through stories, we often encounter new and different experiences; alternatively, the familiar may be made strange or we may experience the unfamiliar in more intimate ways. All of this can provoke reflection and inspire one to consider the feelings and circumstances of others. In highlighting the individuality of each narrator's life and the context of their caring relationships, stories about caregiving have the potential to widen our circle of compassion by eliciting an empathetic response from readers approaching the text from a position of openness, since vulnerability is part of the human condition and we all share a human need for connection. Storytelling provides readers with glimpses of insight into the hopes and needs of others, providing an opportunity to cultivate habits of imaginative identification and empathetic understanding that Hamington and Rosenow claim can help foster a sense of connection to people from different backgrounds, across their embodied differences.[52] The glimpses of insight these stories reveal about the lives and bodies of others provide a nuanced and richer understanding from which to care about them, perhaps prompting readers to think anew about care in their own lives, about how they interpret disability and act toward others.

While affective experiences born out of the demands of care constitute a horizon of commonality, the complexity of caregiving can profoundly affect the perceived "alikeness" between parents. That's because the moral experience of caregiving reflects the practical and existential conflicts parents face. Experiences of caregiving are made intelligible out of what anthropologist Arthur Kleinman describes as the "lived flow of interpersonal experience in an intensely particular local world."[53] For the parents in this book, moral experience is situated at the intersection of justice, power, care, agency, and bodily difference. Shifts in footing between parents within care networks speaks clearly to the differences that make a difference in the continual project of making sense of one's life as an embodied subject embedded in a social, moral, and historical lifeworld.

Moral ambivalence is a component of care that can keep caregivers open to the interminable paths they are set on. Andrew Solomon says, "Asking the parents of severely disabled children to feel less negative emotion than the parents of healthy children is ludicrous.... You cannot decide whether to be ambivalent," he concludes. "All you can decide is what to do with your ambivalence."[54] In light of these insights on endurance and existential hope, we should consider morality as the blurring of vulnerability, care, commitment, loss, exhaustion, pain, and love.

Epilogue

THE SLOW DRIPPING OF TIME

I was expecting a moment of epiphany, where all my uncertainty around caregiving and the lives of my participants would transmogrify into insight, where everything would come together in one clarifying instant. No such moment occurred. My participants didn't speak of any epiphanic moments either. It's the slow dripping of time that changes one's embodied perspective. With the gift of time, I found myself inhabiting my ambivalence toward caregiving more easily.

The men and women I spent time with during fieldwork provided my entrée into the subaltern world of caregiving. Before then, I had felt especially isolated. I read blog posts written by Ethan, Alice, and Paul when Takoda was a baby. And I took personal comfort in their bold testimonies of struggle and love and living life with a difference. As Scot once said, reflecting on how other parents of disabled children might receive his controversial *Salon* piece, "I'll take that splash of cold water now." But I never participated in the online communities I orbited; nor had I experienced any real moments of experiential convergence with them beyond the point of having a child diagnosed with a disability.

Back then, I wasn't sure what to make of parents' unformulated future projects or the ways they seemed to cling to past significances and attachments. The past continued to spill into the present, producing a disruption and experience of disorientation that seemed insurmountable. Often, it seemed the perplexities of caregiving trapped parents in a cyclical revolt, not unlike the kind of complicated grieving that the psychoanalytic theorist Matthew Bowker describes, in which the "lost object is resuscitated in fantasy, repudiated for departing, destroyed by scorn, revived, and revolted against again and again."[1] The disruption occasioned by caregiving seemed to anchor parents in ambivalence, keeping them, I thought, from settling things once and for all.

Their lives, however, testified to things that were not captured by the contents of their online stories. During our time together, hope, commitment, patience, love, vulnerability, ambivalence, and endurance permeated their narratives and occupied the vibrating silences that passed between us. Once I acquired more personal experiences caring for my son and being cared for myself, the narratives and experiences of my study participants resonated with me differently, more strongly. After all, back during fieldwork Takoda was only four years old, and I had never experienced the loss of certainty posed by illness. My experiences since that time have made the silences between things more articulable. That is to say, there were meanings I couldn't or simply wasn't ready to hear at the time.

Structural and interpersonal stigma, as we have already seen—and the cultural meanings attached to disabled bodies—give form and direction to parents' lives. However, at the level of lived experience, we see the ways intimacy, bodily ties, love, and relationships act as a buffer against these prevailing relations of power and corporeal norms. To be sure, with all the moral and practical complexity of caregiving, the parents in this study seemed to share the sentiment that we are answerable to our responsibilities for others and that our own care and freedom have no meaning without reference to the care and freedom of others. Through these merging perspectives and experiences, I came to realize that we live lives of profound interdependence and that two people can create something far greater than either can achieve alone. Indeed, the emergence of meaning in this relational space of intimacy and mutuality is the sacred stuff of existence, the fruit of being.

．　．　．　．　．

We are nearing Lake Garda. The early evening sun is melting into the hills. For now, those dark months of the soul have passed, along with the numbing silence that had entrapped me in such stagnant and depressive despair. Thoughts stir in my mind, some clearer than others, but I'm too tired to inhabit any of them and so there they must remain, in the ether somewhere, as formless potential. The sun slices gold rays across my face and I close my eyes and for the first time in a while there is an aching hope.

Life is happening.

UPDATE 2020

Shortly after New Year 2020, I returned to the United States and caught up with several of the men I came to know during my research. A lot has changed in their lives since then.

Earl and Suzanne helped Zachary transition into a community residential facility. They say he is happy in his new setting and has taken to wearing a shirt and tie—a sign, perhaps, of how grown up he feels. After twenty-seven years of caring for Zachary, they recently took their first overseas trip together to France. Upon returning, Earl retired from the fire department. He and Suzanne moved a short distance away to a horse ranch, where Earl loves to spend his days working with rescued horses.

Doug now cares for Nick full time and is the assistant manager of a local grocery store. The last couple years were marked by hospital stays and group homes, as Doug and his former wife tried their best to manage Nick's violent outbursts. In the end, they decided Nick would be happiest under Doug's full-time care. During my time with them, Nick had a couple of temper outbursts that seemed to arise from feelings of frustration or a desire to regain control over his environment—like when I arrived at his doorstep rather than the case worker he expected. In each instance, Doug very expertly calmed him down, leaning his forehead against Nick's and gently talking to him. On the afternoon of my visit in 2020, Nick held my hand as we wandered the aisles of the grocery store Doug manages, filling our trolley with a variety of his favorite chips.

Sometime last year Paul had a colonoscopy after he noticed blood in his stools. What he thought was probably an internal hemorrhoid ended up being stage IIIC colorectal cancer. He recalls waking up from anesthesia on the hospital gurney and hearing the doctor's thoughts: "It looks to be primary. You will probably need radiation, surgery, and a temporary colostomy." He said the drive home with his wife, Alice, felt like an eternity. He was grappling with the idea that after almost three decades of being a caregiver he was going to be a care *taker*. When he got home the first thing he did was kiss Pearl, after which he retired to the bedroom and ruminated on the worst-case scenario: what will happen to her when I am gone? After radiation therapy, surgery, and chemotherapy, Paul reports that things are looking good. He says he's thankful to be alive, thankful for medical science, regardless of how barbaric it can be, thankful for all the people in his community who brought him food and showed their care, and thankful for Alice's incredible support. Sure, things could be better, he says, but we go on. He's bracing himself for another round of chemotherapy. Anything that ups his long-term survival is worth every bit of discomfort, he said.

On winter solstice last year my son unexpectedly died. We found him in the morning. He'd stopped breathing sometime during the night. In 2011 when he was born, we named him Takoda: a Sioux Amerindian name meaning "friend to all." It was clear from the outpouring of love at his funeral service that we couldn't have chosen a more fitting name for him. There was a soft light in the sky, slowly blending into the deepening evening, as Kim and I drove out to the cremation grounds behind the hearse carrying his body. As we said our final goodbyes, we took comfort in knowing that his gentle and kind spirit had reached so far and so wide across his short life. He was eight.

At the moment it's still hard to imagine what life will look like without him. Among the many things I will miss about him, I will miss his remarkable openness to the world. Many of us go through life only partially engaged with our surroundings and those around us. He was not like this. I rewatched a videotape recently of his sixth birthday party, which we held at a wildlife park. Sitting there in his wheelchair, amid the buzz of familiar family conversation, he heard a bird singing in the background. He tilted his head at the sound of her song and gently smiled.

While writing this epilogue I came across the eulogy I read at his funeral service. There is one section from my letter to him that I would like to share:

> There's a Zulu phrase, *Umuntu ngumuntu ngabantu*, which means "a person is a person through other persons." I want you to know that I am who I am because of you. You taught me to be attentive to the diversity of ways humans inhabit the world. We communicated through our bodies. Through their intertwining I learned that our bodies are the foundation of care and human relatedness. And that these are the foundations of our humanity. Your mummy said the other night, "He loved being him." I want you to know that we loved you being you too. We will always be grateful for the love we shared during your brief stay with us.

We will go on caring for our memories of Takoda. We will aspire to attain his strength and gentle grace for the rest of our lives. If I could tell him one thing, it would be how grateful we are that we were the ones who got to be his mummy and daddy during his brief time with us.

Notes

1. Harbin 2016, xi.

2. It is in terms of such features that I speak of *worlds* within which experience is situated. Our worlds are disclosed in relation to what matters to us given our identities. Therefore, as Dreyfus writes, "we are capable of changing our identities and so our world" (2016, 121). Such worlds, however, are constituted within the world of everyday shared life that we have in common with others. Through our shared cultural practices and acting in the world we come to understand ourselves in the context of our particular culture, time, and place in history with others.

3. Fuchs 2017a, 291.

4. Fuchs 2017a, 312.

5. Fuchs 2017a, 291.

6. Merleau-Ponty 1995, 416.

7. Schutz and Luckman 1973, 159.

8. This form of research is known as autophenomenography. This approach focuses on the researcher's lived experience of a particular phenomenon, in contrast to a focus on their location within a sociocultural context, as is often the case in autoethnography—though these categories are not mutually exclusive (see Allen-Collinson 2016).

9. Kleinman 2010, 17.

10. Ranson 2015, 1.

11. Doucet 2006, 38.

12. Connell and Messerschmidt's structural analysis of power focuses on the hierarchical relations between different groups of men and women, for example, how particular constructs of masculinity and exalted ideals of manhood find expression in social conditions and configurations of gender practice, legitimating the societal dominance of men. For example, ruthless competitiveness, aggression, domination, emotional distance, and economic power, are generally seen as the quickest routes to gender and social ascendency (see 2005, 832 and 850)

13. Freitag 2018.

14. Heidegger 2010, 19.

15. Barrett 1962, 109.

16. In most cases, I was welcomed into their homes and workplaces and welcomed to shadow my research participants for stretches of time, observing them across situations and activities in spaces and times I would not have had access to otherwise; a privilege I attribute to my insider status as a father and caregiver.

17. Jackson 2013, 9; see also Jackson and Piette 2017.

18. Piette 2015, 67.

19. See, for example, Becker 1999, Csordas 1994, and Jackson 2013.

20. Jackson 2013, 63.

21. See Gallagher and Meltzoff 1996.

22. Gallagher and Meltzoff describe the body schema as "a system of motor capacities that function without the necessity of perceptual monitoring" (1996, 3). For Merleau-Ponty (1995), the body schema connects the lived body to a world with meaning and potentiality through the body's situational understanding of space and spatial features.

23. According to the philosopher Martin Heidegger, "being-in-the-world" refers to the way I am always already involved in the world, which is disclosed in my understanding of the world. Furthermore, he uses the term "being-with" for the way we are immersed in a shared world of meaning with others so that understanding others and ourselves is intimately connected (2010: 55, 120, 158). Or, as Nick Crossley writes, "Our lives, thoughts, feelings, and actions are always interwoven with those of others such that they cannot be understood atomistically" (2015: 67).

24. Merleau-Ponty 1995, 352.

25. Of course, as embodied beings we are also influenced by interactions between social and genetic environmental factors.

26. Wahl 1971, 16.

27. Hamington 2004.

28. Existential anthropologist Albert Piette urges the researcher to give detailed attention to what he calls the "minor mode" to trace an individual through time and space (2015, 48).

29. Heidegger 2010, 11.

30. Heidegger 2010, 132.

31. Blattner 2005, 52

32. Othering operates through symbolic and social practices that place misrecognized others outside the realm of social and moral belonging through stereotypes, prejudice, or ignorance.

33. Kittay and Carlson 2010, 411.

34. Kittay 2009, 610.

35. Kittay 2009, 613.

36. Kittay 1999, 29.

37. Kittay 1999, 180.

38. Geertz 1988, 141.

39. Hamington and Rosenow 2019, 103 and 14.

40. Shakespeare 2006: 57.

CHAPTER 2. THE DEPTHS OF TIME

Chapter epigraph: Courtesy of the Society of Authors as the Literary Representative of the Estate of Virginia Woolf

1. Heidegger 2010, 16.

2. See de Wolfe 2013.

3. Heidegger 2010; Merleau-Ponty 1995, 1968.

4. Heidegger 2010, 145; Merleau-Ponty 1995, 22.

5. PDD-NOS would later be folded into an autism spectrum diagnosis in the DSM-V (2013).

6. See Wolff et al. (2016) for more information on this.

7. Kelly 2005, 187.

8. Proust 2003, 70.

9. Brown and Reavey 2015.

10. Brown and Reavey 2015, 26.

11. Brown and Reavey 2015, 26.

12. 1896, cited in Rose 2007, 294.

13. Kohn 2010, 197.

14. Merleau-Ponty 1968.

15. Merleau-Ponty 1968, 248.

16. Merleau-Ponty 1968.

17. Merleau-Ponty 1968, 147.

18. Merleau-Ponty 1968, 268.

19. Usher 2005, 25.

20. Mazis 1992, 56.

21. Merleau-Ponty 1968, 240.

22. Weiss 2008, 19.

23. Merleau-Ponty 1995, 305.

24. Bullington 2013, 24.

25. Bullington 2013, 24.

26. Fuchs 2007.

27. Casey 2000, 147.

28. Fuchs 2011.

29. Fuchs 2012, 15.

30. Fuchs 2012, 9.

31. Merleau-Ponty 1995.

32. Merleau-Ponty 1995, xviii.

33. Merleau-Ponty 1995, xviii.

34. Casey 2000, 155.

35. Mattingly 2010, 43.

36. Frank 2013, 53.

37. Frank 2013, 23.

38. Frank 2013.

39. Frank 2013, 97.

40. Frank 2013, 98.

41. Frank 2013, 98.

42. Frank 2013, 127.

43. Frank 2013, 108.

44. Weiss 2008.

45. In order to ensure Ethan's and Paul's privacy, I have decided not to reference blog posts.

CHAPTER 3. BETWEEN BODIES

1. Greenfeld 1972.

2. Greenfeld 1972, 71.

3. Leder 1990, 32.

4. Hamington 2002, 2004.

5. Hamington 2002.

6. Hamington 2004, 50.

7. Merleau-Ponty 1995, 139.

8. Merleau-Ponty 1995, 139.

9. Kelly 2002, 377.

10. Kelly 2002, 377.

11. Merleau-Ponty 1995, 137.

12. Dreyfus 2007.

13. Merleau-Ponty 1995, 136.

14. Dreyfus 2002, 8.

15. Merleau-Ponty 1995, 429.

16. Gallagher and Meltzoff 1996, 3.

17. Merleau-Ponty 1995, 143.
18. Merleau-Ponty 1995, 143.
19. Merleau-Ponty 1995, 143.
20. See Price 2009, 1.
21. Silberman 2015, 50.
22. Merleau-Ponty 1968, 146.
23. Merleau-Ponty 1968, 147.
24. Maclaren 2014, 99.
25. Maclaren 2014, 99.
26. Maclaren 2014, 100.
27. Merleau-Ponty 1995, 354.
28. Merleau-Ponty 1995, 185.
29. Diprose 2012, 54.
30. Diprose 2012, 54.
31. Merleau-Ponty 1968, 147.
32. Noddings 1986, 23.
33. Noddings 1986, 23.
34. Noddings 1986, 14.
35. Kittay 1999, 38.
36. Merleau-Ponty 1995, 229.
37. Merleau-Ponty 1995, 230.
38. Heidegger 2010, 158.
39. Merleau-Ponty 1995, 229.
40. Grandin 2011.
41. Grandin 1996.
42. Hanlon 2012, 137.
43. Solomon 2014, 362.
44. Pallasmaa 2014, 243.
45. Fuchs 2017b.
46. Fuchs 2017b, 16.
47. Daly 2016, 211.
48. Erskine 2015, 45.
49. Griffiths and Smith 2016.
50. Griffiths and Smith 2016, 133.
51. Griffiths and Smith 2016, 133.
52. Fuchs and Koch 2014, 5.
53. Fuchs and Koch 2014, 6, emphasis in the original.
54. Daly 2016.
55. Hamington 2015, 289.
56. Hamington 2004, 64.

CHAPTER 4. CONDITIONS OF POSSIBILITY

1. Heidegger 2010, 145.
2. Merleau-Ponty 1995, 455.
3. Heidegger 2010, 19.
4. Heidegger 2010, 141.
5. Alcoff 2006.
6. See Heidegger 2010, 145.
7. Alcoff 2006, 95.
8. Alcoff 2006, 5.
9. Merleau-Ponty 1995, 446.
10. hooks 2004.
11. hooks 2004, 18.
12. Eldredge 2011.
13. Eldredge 2011, 12.
14. Eldredge 2011, 142.
15. Eldredge 2004, 15.
16. Alcoff 2006, 103.
17. Eldredge 2017.
18. Diehl 2016.
19. McDowell 2015, 29, emphasis added.
20. Zigon 2007, 137.
21. Zigon 2007, 137.
22. Zigon 2007, 138.
23. Schwalbe 2014, 104.
24. Schwalbe 2014, 115.
25. See, for example, Macintyre 1999.
26. White 2008, 32.
27. White 2008, 32.
28. Tronto 1993, 121.
29. Kohn and McKechnie 1999, 3–4.
30. Hanlon 2012, 98.
31. Hanlon 2012, 98.
32. Hanlon 2012, 98.
33. Hanlon 2012, 98.
34. Kittay 1999, x.
35. hooks 2004, 27.
36. hooks 2004.
37. de Beauvoir 2011, 403.
38. de Beauvoir 2011, 403.
39. Noriega 2014, 143.
40. This is known as "stimming": Repetitive, self-stimulating behavior.

41. Nietzsche 1974, 36.

42. Zigon 2007, 138.

CHAPTER 5. BELONGING AND BEING-FOR-OTHERS

1. Sometimes referred to as an Individual Education Plan, or Individual Learning Plan.

2. Wendell 1996, 88.

3. Wendell 1996, 88.

4. Wendell 1996, 88.

5. Wendell 1996, 88.

6. Noonan 2012.

7. Kristeva 2010.

8. Kristeva 2010, 251, emphasis in the original.

9. Kristeva 2010, 251.

10. Grosz 1996, 57.

11. See Alcoff 2006, 185.

12. Alcoff 2006, 216.

13. Merleau-Ponty 1964, 153.

14. Diprose 2002, 54.

15. An alternative assessment is offered to those with disabilities. The No Child Left Behind Act (NCLB) was signed into law in 2002 and was a reauthorization of the previous Elementary and Secondary Education Act (ESEA). NCLB supported standards-based education reform which was intended to raise academic achievement for all students in the K-12 population and "close the achievement gap between poor, inner-city schools and schools in middle-class suburban areas" (Bryant et al. 2015, 22). Aligned with the goal of annual progress, the law mandated that students, including those with disabilities, take annual assessments in reading/language, arts, and arithmetic. Schools and school districts dependent on federal funding were held accountable for eliminating the achievement gap and raising academic achievement.

16. Federal income supplement administered by the Social Security Administration (SSA) for individuals with disabilities with limited income.

17. Special education advocates help parents navigate the special education system, attain special education services, and achieve their child's educational rights. A special education surrogate parent is a person appointed to act in the interest of someone who is without a parent or guardian to oversee their educational rights, usually someone in a residential setting.

18. Lewis 1995, 34.

19. Lewis 1995, 34.

20. Lewis 1995, 34.

21. Lewis 1995, 34.

22. Lewis 1995, 34.

23. Sartre 1992, 461.

24. See Sartre 1992, 462.

25. See Sartre 1992, 355.

26. See Hubert Dreyfus (2016) for a discussion on ethical expertise.

27. Merleau-Ponty 1964, 26.

28. Nussbaum 2004, 184.

29. See Murray and Trevarthen 1985.

30. Trevarthen and Aitken 2001.

31. Trevarthen and Aitken 2001, 20.

32. Maibom 2010, 587.

33. Mackay 2014.

34. Ahmed 2014, 212.

35. Dreyfus 2016, 191.

36. Dreyfus 2016, 191.

37. Dreyfus 2016, 190.

38. Pick 2011, 85.

CHAPTER 6. THE AXIOM OF EQUALITY

1. Shuman 2011, 155.

2. Rapp and Ginsburg 2011, 398; 2001, 537.

3. Rapp and Ginsburg 2001, 534.

4. Shuman 2011, 155.

5. Shuman 2011, 167.

6. Shuman 2011, 167.

7. Shuman 2011, 170.

8. Buber 2000.

9. Buber 2000, 26.

10. Buber 2000, 23.

11. Buber 2000, 26.

12. Hatab 2000, 57.

13. Rosenfield 1992, 141.

14. See, for example, Carpenter and Towers 2008; Rendall 1997.

15. Featherstone 1980, 41.

16. Williams 1997, 2.

17. Williams 1997, 2.

18. In the last chapter I spoke about historically inherited perceptual practices of identification and classification that shape how we relate to others and produce forms of social exclusion.

19. Sesame Workshop is an American nonprofit educational organization responsible for educational and social impact programs.

20. Julia was introduced to the mainstream show in 2017, in episode 4715.
21. Dell'Antonia 2015.
22. Sea 2003.
23. Hacking 2009.
24. Sea 2003.
25. Hacking 2009.
26. See, for instance, Belek 2017.
27. Silberman 2015, 59.
28. Tran and Anton 2002.
29. Parsons 2002.
30. Silberman 2015, 59.
31. Sea 2003.
32. Harris 2015.
33. Hamington and Rosenow 2019, 13.
34. [GreggBeratan] 2017, February 23.
35. Clifford and Marcus 1986.
36. Hatab 1997, 411.
37. Koselleck 2004, 257.
38. Pettit 2004.
39. Meyer 1956, 29.
40. Meyer 1956, 29.
41. Peace 2014.
42. See, for instance, Ratcliffe (2015) for a discussion on existential hope.
43. Ratcliffe 2015, 123.
44. Camus 2005, 26.
45. Ratcliffe 2015, 103.
46. Ratcliffe 2015, 109.
47. Garcia 2014, 59.
48. Heidegger 2010, 120.
49. Frank 2013, 49.
50. Hamington and Rosenow 2019, 73.
51. Hamington and Rosenow 2019, 8.
52. Hamington and Rosenow 2019, 51.
53. Kleinman 1997, 53.
54. Solomon 2014, 402.

EPILOGUE

1. Bowker 2011, 173.

References

Ahmed, S. 2014. *The Cultural Politics of Emotion*. 2nd ed. Edinburgh: Edinburgh University Press.

Alcoff, L. 2006. *Visible Identities: Race, Gender, and the Self*. Oxford: Oxford University Press.

Allen-Collinson, J. 2016. "Autoethnography as Engagement." In *Handbook of Autoethnography*, edited by S. H. Jones, T. E. Adams, and C. Ellis, 281–99. New York: Routledge.

American Psychiatric Association 2013. *Diagnostic and Statistical Manual of Mental Disorders* (5th ed.). Arlington, VA: American Psychiatric Publishing.

Barrett, W. 1962. *Irrational Man: A Study in Existential Philosophy*. New York: Anchor Books.

de Beauvoir, S. (1949) 2011. *The Second Sex*. Translated by C. Borde and S. Malovany-Chevallier. London: Vintage.

Becker, G. 1999. *Disrupted Lives: How People Create Meaning in a Chaotic World*. Berkeley: University of California Press.

Belek, B. 2017. "I Feel Therefore I Matter: Emotional Rhetoric and Autism Self-Advocacy." *Anthropology Now* 9, no. 2 (September): 57–69.

Blattner, W. 2005. *Heidegger's Temporal Idealism*. Cambridge, UK: Cambridge University Press.

Bowker, M. H. 2011. "The Meaning of Absurd Protest: The Book of Job, Albert Camus, and C. Fred Alford's After the Holocaust." *Journal of Psycho-Social Studies* 5, no. 1 (January): 163–83.

Brown, S. D., and P. Reavey. 2015. *Vital Memories and Affect: Living with a Difficult Past*. New York: Routledge.

Buber, M. 2000. *I and Thou*. New York: Scribner.

Bullington, J. 2013. *The Expression of the Psychosomatic Body from a Phenomenological Perspective*. London: Springer.

Camus, A. (1942) 2005. *The Myth of Sisyphus*. London: Penguin.

Carpenter, B., and C. Towers. 2008. "Recognising Fathers: The Needs of Fathers of Children with Disabilities." *Support for Learning* 23, no. 3 (July): 118–25.

Casey, E. S. 2000. *Remembering: A Phenomenological Study*. Indianapolis: Indiana University Press.

Clifford, J., and G. E. Marcus, eds. 1986. *Writing Culture: The Poetics and Politics of Ethnography*. Berkeley: University of California Press.

Connell, R. W., and J. W. Messerschmidt. 2005. "Hegemonic Masculinity: Rethinking the Concept." *Gender and Society* 19, no. 6 (December): 829–59.

Crossley, N. (2015). "Relational Sociology and Culture: A Preliminary Framework." *International Review of Sociology* 25, no. 1:65–85.

Csordas, T. 1994. *Embodiment and Experience: The Existential Ground of Culture and Self*. Cambridge, UK: Cambridge University Press.

Daly, A. 2016. *Merleau-Ponty and the Ethics of Intersubjectivity*. London: Palgrave MacMillan.

Dell'Antonia, K. J. 2015. "Sesame Street Has a New Character with Autism. Will Kids without It Ever See Her?" *New York Times*, October 22, 2015. https://parenting.blogs.nytimes.com/2015/10/22/sesame-street-has-a-new-character-with-autism-will-typical-children-ever-see-her/.

Diehl, H. A. 2016. "Breaking Dad: Reimagining Postwar Models of American Fatherhood in *Breaking Bad*." In *Pops in Pop Culture: Fatherhood, Masculinity, and the New Man*, edited by E. Podnieks, 179–94. New York: Pelgrave.

Diprose, R. 2012. *Corporeal Generosity: On Giving with Nietzsche, Merleau-Ponty, and Levinas*. New York: SUNY.

Doucet, A. 2006. *Do Men Mother? Fathering, Care, and Domestic Responsibility*. Toronto: University of Toronto Press.

Dreyfus, H. L. 2002. "A Phenomenology of Skill Acquisition as the Basis for a Merleau-Pontian Non-Representationalist Cognitive Science." Berkeley: Department of Philosophy, University of California. https://philarchive.org/archive/DREAPO.

———. 2007. "Why Heideggerian AI Failed and How Fixing It Would Require Making It More Heideggerian." *Philosophical Psychology* 20, no. 2 (April): 247–68.

———. 2016. *Skillful Coping: Essays on the Phenomenology of Everyday Perception and Action*. New York: Oxford University Press.

Eldredge, J. 2004. *You Have What It Takes: What Every Father Needs to Know*. Nashville: Thomas Nelson.

———. 2011. *Wild at Heart: Discovering the Secret of a Man's Soul*. Nashville: Thomas Nelson.

———. 2017. "How Women Can Help Men Steal Back Their Masculinity with John Elridge." By D. Partridge. Podcast, May 2017. http://startupcamp.com /podcast/women-can-help-men-steal-back-masculinity-john-eldredge/.

Erskine, R. G. 2015. *Relational Patterns, Therapeutic Presence: Concepts and Practice of Integrative Psychotherapy*. London: Karnac Books.

Featherstone, H. 1980. *A Difference in the Family*. New York: Basic Books.

Frank, A. 2013. *The Wounded Storyteller: Body, Illness and Ethics*. 2nd ed. Chicago: University of Chicago Press.

Freitag, L. 2018. *Extreme Caregiving: The Moral Work of Raising Children with Special Needs*. New York: Oxford University Press.

Fuchs, T. 2007. "Psychotherapy of the Lived Space: A Phenomenological and Ecological Concept." American Journal of Psychotherapy 61, no. 4: 423–439.

Fuchs, T. 2011. "Body Memory and the Unconscious." In *Founding Psycho- analysis: Phenomenological Theory of Subjectivity and the Psychoanalytical Experience*, edited by D. Lohmar and J. Brudzinska, 69–82.

———. 2012. "The Phenomenology of Body Memory." In *Body Memory, Metaphor and Movement*, edited by T. Fuchs, S. C. Koch, C. Müller, and M. Summa, 9–22. Philadelphia: John Benjamins.

———. 2017a. "Self Across Time: The Diachronic Unity of Bodily Existence." *Phenomenology and the Cognitive Sciences* 16:291–315.

———. 2017b. "Intercorporeality and Interaffectivity." In *Intercorporeality: Emerging Socialities in Interaction*, edited by C. Meyer, J. Streeck, and J. S. Jordan, 3–22. Oxford: Oxford University Press.

Fuchs, T., and S. C. Koch. 2014. "Embodied Affectivity: On Moving and Being Moved." *Frontiers in Psychology* 5:508.

Gallagher, S., and A. N. Meltzoff. 1996. "The Earliest Sense of Self and Others: Merleau-Ponty and Recent Developmental Studies." *Philosophical Psychology* 9, no. 2 (March): 211–33.

Garcia, A. 2014. "The Promise: On the Morality of the Marginal and the Illicit." *Ethos* 42, no. 1 (March): 51–64.

Geertz, C. 1988. *Work and Lives: The Anthropologist as Author*. Stanford: Stanford University Press.

Grandin, T. 1996. "My Experiences with Visual Thinking, Sensory Problems and Communication Difficulties." Centre for the Study of Autism.https://www .autism.org/temple-grandin-inside-asd/.

———. 2011. *The Way I See it: A Personal Look at Autism & Asperger's*. Arlington, TX: Future Horizons.

Greenfeld, J. 1972. *A Child Called Noah: A Family Journal*. New York: Holt, Rinehart and Winston.

Griffiths, C., and M. Smith. 2016. "Attuning: A Communication Process between

People with Severe and Profound Intellectual Disability and Their Interaction Partners." *Journal of Applied Research in Intellectual Disabilities* 29, no. 2 (March): 124–38.

Grosz, E. 1996. "Intolerable Ambiguity: Freaks as/at the Limit." In *Freakery: Cultural Spectacles of the Extraordinary Body*, edited by R. Thomson, 55–68. New York: New York University Press.

Hacking, I. 2009. "Autistic Autobiography." *Philosophical Transactions of the Royal Society B: Biological Sciences* 364, no. 1522 (May): 1467–73.

Hamington, M. 2002. "A Father's Touch: Caring Embodiment and a Moral Revolution." In *Revealing Male Bodies*, edited by N. Tuana, W. Cowling, and M. Hamington, 269–85. Bloomington: Indiana University Press.

———. 2004. *Embodied Care: Jane Adams, Maurice Merleau-Ponty, and Feminist Ethics*. Chicago: University of Illinois Press.

———. 2015. "Politics Is Not a Game: The Radical Potential of Care." In *Care Ethics and Political Theory*, edited by D. Engster and M. Hamington, 272–91. Oxford: Oxford University Press.

Hamington, M., and C. Rosenow. 2019. *Care Ethics and Poetry*. Cham: Palgrave Macmillan.

Hanlon, N. 2012. *Masculinities, Care and Equality: Identity and Nurture in Men's Lives*. New York: Palgrave Macmillan.

Harbin, A. 2016. "Bodily Disorientation and Moral Change." *Hypatia* 27, no. 2 (Spring): 261–80.

Harris, R. L. 2015. "A Range of Reactions to Airline's Removal of Autistic Child." *New York Times*, May 14, 2015. https://www.nytimes.com/2015/05/14/travel/a-range-of-reactions-to-airlines-removal-of-autistic-child.html.

Hatab, L. J. 1997. "Ethics and Finitude: Heideggerian Contributions to Moral Philosophy." Paper presented at the University of Chicago After Postmodernism conference, Chicago.

———. 2000. *Ethics and Finitude: Heideggerian Contributions to Moral Philosophy*. New York: Rowman and Littlefield.

Heidegger, M. (1927) 2010. *Being and Time*. Translated by J. Stambaugh. Albany: State University of New York Press.

hooks, b. 2004. *The Will to Change: Men, Masculinity, and Love*. New York: Washington Square.

Jackson, M. 2013. *Lifeworlds: Essays in Existential Anthropology*. Chicago: University of Chicago Press.

Jackson, M., and A. Piette, eds. 2017. *What Is Existential Anthropology*. New York: Berghahn.

Kelly, S. D. 2002. "Merleau-Ponty on the Body." *Ratio* 15, no. 4 (December): 376–91.

Kelly, S. E. 2005. "A Different Light: Examining Impairment through Parent

Narratives of Childhood Disability." *Journal of Contemporary Ethnography* 34, no. 2 (April): 180–205.

Kittay, E. 1999. *Love's Labor: Essays on Women, Equality, and Dependency*. New York: Routledge.

———. 2009. "The Personal Is Philosophical Is Political: A Philosopher and Mother of a Cognitively Disabled Person Sends Notes from the Battlefield." *Metaphilosophy* 40, nos. 3–4 (July): 606–27.

Kittay, E. F., and L. Carlson, eds. 2010. *Cognitive Disability and Its Challenge to Moral Philosophy*. Massachusetts: Wiley-Blackwell.

Kleinman, A. 1997. *Writing at the Margin: Discourse between Anthropology and Medicine*. Berkeley: University of California Press.

———. 2010. "The Divided Meaning of Being Human." In *Rethinking the Human*, edited by J. M. Molina, D. K. Swearer, and S. L. McGarry, 17–30. Massachusetts: Harvard Divinity School.

Kohn, T. 2010. "The Role of Serendipity and Memory in Experiencing Fields." In *The Ethnographic Self as Resource*, edited by P. Collins and A. Gallinat, 185–99. Oxford: Berghahn.

Kohn, T., and R. McKechnie, eds. 1999. *Extending the Boundaries of Care: Medical Ethics & Caring Practices*. Oxford: Berg.

Koselleck, R. 2004. *Futures Past: On the Semantics of Historical Time*. Translated by K. Tribe. New York: Columbia University Press.

Kristeva, J. 2010. *Hatred and Forgiveness*. New York: Columbia University Press.

Leder, D. 1990. *The Absent Body*. Chicago: University of Chicago Press.

Lewis, M. 1995. *Shame: The Exposed Self*. New York: Free Press.

Macintyre, S. 1999. *A Concise History of Australia*. Cambridge, UK: Cambridge University Press.

Mackay, H. 2014. *The Art of Belonging*. Sydney: Macmillan.

Maclaren, K. 2014. "Touching Matters: Embodiments of Intimacy." *Emotion, Space and Society* 13 (November): 95–102.

Maibom, H. 2010. "The Descent of Shame." *Philosophy and Phenomenological Research* 80, no. 3 (May): 566–94.

Mattingly, C. 2010. *The Paradox of Hope: Journeys through a Clinical Borderland*. Berkeley: University of California Press.

Mazis, G. 1992. "Merleau-Ponty and the Backward Flow of Time." In *Merleau-Ponty, Hermeneutics and Postmodernism*, edited by T. W. Busch, and S. Gallagher, 53–68. Albany: State University of New York Press.

McDowell, T. 2015. *Applying Critical Social Theories to Family Therapy Practice*. New York: Springer.

Merleau-Ponty, M. (1945) 1995. *Phenomenology of Perception*. Translated by C. Smith, New York: Routledge.

———. 1964. *The Primacy of Perception*. Translated by William Cobb and edited by James M. Edie. Evanston: Northwestern University Press.

———. (1964) 1968. *The Visible and the Invisible*. Translated by A. Lingis. Evanston: Northwestern University Press.

Meyer, L. 1956. *Emotion and Meaning in Music*. Chicago: University of Chicago Press.

Murray, L., and C. Trevarthen. 1985. "Emotional Regulation of Interactions between Two-Month-Olds and Their Mothers." In *Social Perceptions in Infants*, edited by T. M. Field and N. A. Fox, 177–97. Norwood: Ablex.

Nietzsche, F. (1882) 1974. *The Gay Science*. New York: Vintage Books.

Noddings, N. 1986. *Caring: A Feminine Approach to Ethics and Moral Education*. 2nd ed. Berkeley: University of California Press.

Noonan, T. 2012. "A Father's Love." *Yahoo 7*, September 2, 2012. https://au.news.yahoo.com/sunday-night/features/a/14716802/a-fathers-love/.

Noriega, G. N. 2014. *Just between Us: An Ethnography of Male Identity and Intimacy in Rural Communities of Northern Mexico*. Tucson: University of Arizona Press.

Nussbaum, M. C. 2004. *Hiding from Humanity: Disgust, Shame and the Law*. Princeton: Princeton University Press.

Pallasmaa, J. 2014. "Space, Place and Atmosphere: Emotion and Peripheral Perception in Architectural Experience." *Lebenswelt: Aesthetics and Philosophy of Experience* 4, no. 1 (July): 230–45.

Parsons, D. 2002. "Looking at a Murder for What It Really Is." *Los Angeles Times*, August 2, 2002. http://articles.latimes.com/2002/aug/02/local/me-parsons2.

Peace, W. 2014. "More on Our Failure to Educate People about Disability." *Bad Cripple* (blog), July 13, 2014. http://badcripple.blogspot.com.au/2014/07/more-on-our-failure-to-educate-people.html.

Pettit, P. 2004. "Hope and Its Place in Mind." *Annals of the American Academy of Political and Social Science* 592 (March): 152–56.

Pick, A. 2011. *Creaturely Poetics: Animality and Vulnerability in Literature and Film*. New York: Columbia University Press.

Piette, A. 2015. *Existence in the Details: Theory and Methodology in Existential Anthropology*. Berlin: Duncker & Humblot.

Price, M. S. 2009. *The Special Needs Child and Divorce: A Practical Guide to Evaluating and Handling Cases*. Chicago: ABA.

Proust, M. (1913) 2003. *Swann's Way*. Translated by C. K. Scott-Moncrieff, T. Kilmartin, and D. J. Enright. New York: The Modern Library.

Ranson, G. 2015. *Fathering, Masculinity and the Embodiment of Care*. New York: Palgrave Macmillan.

Rapp, R., and F. Ginsburg. 2001. "Enabling Disability: Rewriting Kinship, Reimagining Citizenship." *Public Culture* 13, no. 3 (Fall): 533–56.

———. 2011. "Reverberations: Disability and the New Kinship Imaginary." *Anthropological Quarterly* 84, no. 2 (Spring): 379–410.

Ratcliffe, M. 2015. *Experiences of Depression: A Study in Phenomenology*. Oxford: Oxford University Press.

Rendall, D. 1997. "Fatherhood and Learning Disabilities: A Personal Account of Reaction and Resolution." *Journal of Learning Disabilities for Nursing Health and Social Care* 1, no. 2 (June): 77–83.

Rose, S. H. 2007. *Oedipal Rejection: Echoes in the Relationships of Gay Men*. Youngstown: Cambria.

Rosenfield, I. 1992. *The Strange, Familiar, and Forgotten: An Anatomy of Consciousness*. New York: Vintage Books.

Sartre, J-P. (1943) 1992. *Being and Nothingness*. New York: Washington Square.

Schutz, A., and T. Luckmann. 1973. *The Structures of the Lifeworld*, vol. 1. Evanston, IL: Northwestern University Press.

Schwalbe, M. 2014. *Manhood Acts: Gender and the Practices of Domination*. Boulder: Paradigm.

Sea, S. 2003. "Planet Autism." *Salon*, September 27, 2003. https://www.salon.com/2003/09/27/autism_8/.

Shakespeare, T. 2006. *Disability Rights and Wrongs*. Abingdon: Routledge.

Shuman, A. 2011. "On the Verge: Phenomenology and Empathetic Unsettlement." *Journal of American Folklore* 124, no. 493 (Summer): 147–74.

Silberman, S. 2015. *NeuroTribes: The Legacy of Autism and the Future of Neurodiversity*. New York: Avery.

Solomon, A. 2014. *Far from the Tree: Parents, Children and the Search for Identity*. London: Vintage.

Tran, M., and M. Anton. 2002. "Stress Pushed Man to Kill Son, Himself, Family Says." *Los Angeles Times*, July 31, 2002. http://articles.latimes.com/2002/jul/31/local/me-bodies31.

Trevarthen, C., and K. J. Aitken. 2001. "Infant Intersubjectivity: Research, Theory and Clinical Applications." *Journal of Child Psychology and Psychiatry* 42, no. 1 (January): 3–48.

Tronto, J. 1993. *Moral Boundaries: A Political Argument for an Ethic of Care*. New York: Routledge.

Usher, R. 2005. "The Story of the Self: Education, Experience and Autobiography." In *Biography and Education: A Reader*, edited by M. Erben, 20–34. New York: Routledge.

Wahl, J. 1971. *A Short History of Existentialism*. Connecticut: Greenwood Press.

Weiss, G. 2008. *Refiguring the Ordinary*. Indianapolis: Indiana University Press.

Wendell, S. 1996. *The Rejected Body: Feminist Philosophical Reflections on Disability*. New York: Routledge.

White, A. M. 2008. *Ain't I a Feminist? African American Men Speak Out on Fatherhood, Friendship, Forgiveness, and Freedom*. New York: State University of New York Press.

Williams, P. 1997. *Seeing a Color-Blind Future: The Paradox of Race.* New York: Farrar, Straus and Giroux.

de Wolfe, J. 2013. "Parents Speak: An Ethnographic Study of Autism Parents." PhD diss., Columbia University.

Wolff, J. L., B. C. Spillman, V. A. Freedman, and J. D. Kasper. 2016. "A National Profile of Family and Unpaid Caregivers Who Assist Older Adults with Health Care Activities." *JAMA Internal Medicine,* 176, no. 3 (March): 372–79.

Woolf, V. 1998. *Orlando.* Oxford: Oxford University Press.

Zigon, J. 2007. "Moral Breakdown and the Ethical Demand." *Anthropological Theory* 7, no. 2 (June): 131–50.

Index

Founded in 1893,
UNIVERSITY OF CALIFORNIA PRESS
publishes bold, progressive books and journals
on topics in the arts, humanities, social sciences,
and natural sciences—with a focus on social
justice issues—that inspire thought and action
among readers worldwide.

The UC PRESS FOUNDATION
raises funds to uphold the press's vital role
as an independent, nonprofit publisher, and
receives philanthropic support from a wide
range of individuals and institutions—and from
committed readers like you. To learn more, visit
ucpress.edu/supportus.

8/2021